Fervent Prayer

Patricia Marlett

Fervent Prayer
Copyright © 2018, 2022 by Patricia Marlett
All rights reserved.

No part of this publication may be reproduced, stored in a retrieval system or transmitted in any way by any means, electronic, mechanical, photocopy, recording or otherwise without the prior permission of the author except as provided by USA copyright law.

Scriptures from the King James Bible
Published in the United States of America
Published by High Tower Publishing

First Edition - 2018   ISBN: 978-0-9994680-3-6
Second Edition - 2022   ISBN: 978-0-9994680-3-6

High Tower Publishing
2 Samuel 22:3

ACKNOWLEDGEMENT

I will always, and forevermore, acknowledge and give thanks to God. I honor, praise and give the glory to my heavenly Father; for it is by His grace, that I am blessed. He is my inspiration and with the gift He has bestowed upon me, I write in His honor to glorify His name.

Also, deep appreciation to my husband, Mark, for his unwavering love, support, and dedication he gives as I pursue my passion. You are my rock, I love you.

DEDICATION

This book is dedicated to all who seek answers.

TABLE OF CONTENT

Note from the Author _____ 11

Preface _____ 14

A Fervent Prayer _____ 16

A Marriage Gift _____ 44

Trinity of the Kingdom _____ 57

Communion in Christ _____ 75

Power of Prayer _____ 83

Prayer to the Father _____ 87

Portrait of Man _____ 91

Summary _____ 93

Scriptures _____ 95

Excerpt: Children in the Crossfire _____ 107

Excerpt: Everlasting Love, God's Greatest Gift ___ 109

Note from the Author

If any man speak, let him speak as the oracles of God; if any man minister, let him do it as of the ability which God giveth: that God in all things may be glorified through Jesus Christ, to whom be praise and dominion for ever and ever. Amen.
1 Peter 4:11

It is with honor and glory to our heavenly Father that I take great pleasure in presenting this book to share the truth of God's Word as taught in the Scriptures, and to assure each person who reads the content on the following pages that everything God created and provided is for you.

It has always been about you when God established the foundation of all His creation as we read in the Bible and continues throughout eternity. I hope you gain insight of how much you are truly loved, and how desirous the Father is for you to be with Him today and forever.

God made all things possible through His Son, Jesus, when He gave man a new and better covenant. As a beneficiary of this testament, one of the many gifts is the free will to personally decide if we want a life with Him, one that is eternal. Though it is by our choice, God wants all His children to come home to the Kingdom of

Heaven. We can be with our Father this very moment, spiritually, if we become one in spirit with His Son, Jesus. The first step is a desire to have a relationship with God and become a born-again child of the Father. In Christ, we are changed from a sinner to a saint and secured as a joint-heir through Jesus in the Kingdom.

I pray you are inspired to seek God and accept His Word as the guidepost for your life and maintain a relationship with your heavenly Father. Not simply know of Him, but fall in love with Him, learn His nature and understand what He has done for you, and what He expects of you, His child.

As a child to the parent, we should want our Father's love and a close bond with Him more than anything, ever. Only God can heal a broken body whether it is physical or emotional, only God can supply for personal and professional prosperity, and only God can give us eternal life. There is absolutely nothing permanent on this planet as this earthen place will one day be made anew to receive the New Jerusalem which will be the eternal home of every believer.

God's love, mercy, and grace are forever present and will always protect and provide for His children. We are His most precious creation, made in His likeness, for His pleasure, never forgotten or forsaken. Promises, blessings, gifts, and power are within His Kingdom, and we are personally responsible to acquire the knowledge that God has set forth in His Word, so that we may partake of these Kingdom treasures.

It is vital to understand the role of Christ and His purpose in fulfilling the Father's plan and to accept the Holy Spirit as our tutor who teaches the things of God and is our advocate in the Kingdom. This is crucial to living in the spirit and receiving what He has prepared for you.

There will appear a redundancy within this book, for when speaking of God, the Son, and the Holy Spirit, all are God; and yet, He presents Himself as separate personages for man's purpose. Therefore, each section may have a repetitive thought for the sole purpose of expressing the importance of God and His Kingdom of Heaven. However, a conscious effort has been made to keep the redundancy to a minimum.

With forethought, there are Scriptures appropriately placed to serve as a reference to what God's Word says as the focus is always on His truth. The Scriptures may be applicable more than once.

Our relationship with our heavenly Father is defined in our belief, trust, and unwavering faith. We are not lost souls wandering aimlessly and helpless throughout this life, but saints made righteous and holy in Christ for the Father.

Preface

Call unto me, and I will answer thee, and show thee great and mighty things, which thou knowest not.
James 33:3

*F*ervent *Prayer* gives insight to the most frequently asked question among Christians today. When we pray and an answer doesn't seem to be forthcoming, what has happened? With our human nature, we take the mindset that God is not going to answer our plea; however, this is far from the truth. The Father is always providing for His children.

To obtain an answer to anything we ask of our heavenly Father, it is imperative to have knowledge of how we may ask. As any parent expects their child to ask in a certain manner, so does our heavenly Father. The question becomes are we approaching God with a carnal thought, or as a spirit person born of His Son? Are you privy to the supernatural power of the Holy Spirit within your heart knowing that what you ask, He will do for you?

It's important to understand that everything within the Kingdom of Heaven is Spirit; and therefore, we come before our Father born into His Kingdom even though we remain in an earthen environment.

The resolutions we seek from God are provided through the third person of the Trinity of God, the Holy Spirit, who is the dunamis power of God. Pray as a spirit person and allow the Holy Spirit to intercede and answer your prayers, for He is the provider of what you seek.

God does not withhold His blessings from His children. Our heavenly Father knows of our request before we utter the first word in prayer. He desires to give to His children, for everything within the Kingdom of Heaven is for you. However, we must know how to appropriate our prayers to receive. We are righteous in Christ, and one fervent prayer is all the Father desires.

Pray intimately with much thanksgiving and believe that what you have asked has already been given, while your faith assures you that your heavenly Father has provided.

A FERVENT PRAYER

The effectual fervent prayer of a righteous man availeth much.
James 5:16

The most sought after answer for the number one question asked among Christians today is why are prayers not always answered? Why is it when we pray and sometimes even gather prayer warriors, family, and friends to assist, there seemingly remains no answer from God?

Could our methodology to praying in actuality be in opposition to what God instructs; and thus, hindering our receiving an answer. Is it possible we are obstructing our own prayers. Are we more mindful to pray as we think we should rather than following the instructions given by our heavenly Father. Something to seriously ponder.

Surely, our ceaseless praying should render a response. After all, we have brought forth a plethora of people to make sure our prayers are heard. If we pray long enough, hard enough, and with much deliberation, it should garner God's attention and He will have to oblige because we show such diligence in our efforts. This is man's way, not the Father's instructions. Our prayers are important to God; however, more is not always better especially when it comes to the principles concerning the Kingdom of Heaven. It doesn't place us any closer to God.

We are missing a vital element of God's Kingdom precepts when we think our way is better than what God has said. If our thought is to help God with a gathering of people, we are seriously misunderstanding His Word. Is it wrong to ask others to pray on our behalf? Not at all; however, their prayers should be spoken as God instructs, privately.

Webster's dictionary defines prayer as a solemn request for help, or expression of thanks addressed to God or an object of worship. Therefore, a prayer is a means of communicating to God for the expressed purpose of asking, thanking, and also in daily fellowship with Him.

Our Father informs us exactly how we may come to Him, and He is very specific on this matter. God only requires one thing concerning prayers. He tells us to find a quiet place and speak to Him personally; an intimate time alone with Him. *But thou, when thou prayest, enter into thy closet, and when thou hast shut thy door, <u>pray to thy Father which is in secret</u>; and thy Father which seeth in secret shall <u>reward thee</u> openly.* Matthew 6:6

These are the very words Jesus spoke to His disciples before He would leave them. His command is very straightforward and remains true today, for God's Word is constant, unchanging. God, Himself, is telling us how to approach Him; therefore, Jesus was speaking the Father's Word.

It appears the problem is within man, for we have an innate tendency to manipulate the Word of God to satisfy our perceived expectations. With our human thought and reliance on our fellow man, we adhere to the belief that the more people we gather together in prayer, the better the opportunity of an answer. Our traditional doctrines teach of implementing *prayer warriors* which is not the Father's spoken Word, but man's attempt to show faith.

If we continue to abide by man's specifications and not God's Word, then we need to be prepared for not receiving that which we ask. God already knows what's in our heart, what we have need of; therefore, the prayer isn't to gain His attention but is for our benefit. *Be not ye therefore like unto them; <u>for your Father knoweth what things ye have need of, before ye ask him</u>.* Matthew 6:8

Prayer is teaching us how to be dependent on God, to trust and rely solely on Him. Remember, He already knows what we will present; therefore, how we approach God is crucial to receiving. Our Father doesn't want us begging and pleading but rather find a quiet place when we speak with Him. He wants His children to come to Him with a trustworthy heart and mind thoughtful to His Word with steadfast faith knowing He is the One who has the answers we seek.

Once we have spoken to God about our problem, we are to leave the matter with Him and not interfere by attempting to handle the situation. We do not worry or become anxious, but have a heart of peace accepting that the problem has been resolved. All we are required to do is wait for the manifestation. When we rest in

God's promise with a stance of letting go and letting God's power flow, we have manifested our faith. Any other position is one of unbelief and will negate His power. We can get in the way of our prayers.

For example, when people came to Jesus, they asked of Him personally, and typically, it was for a healing or a raising of the dead. In most cases, there were others present to hear the plea; however, they weren't gathered in prayer pleading and coercing Jesus to render a miracle. He answered the *one fervent prayer of the person in faith doing the asking.* There are many instances but consider the Centurion, or the woman with the issue of blood.

There were times when Jesus had to leave the town in order to heal, for the unbelief of the people therein. *And he took the blind man by the hand, and led him out of the town; and when he had spit on his eyes, and put his hands upon him, he asked him if he saw ought.* Mark 8:23 Though we may think others are praying in faith on our behalf, if there is doubt (unbelief), then it has voided the results. It can be detrimental to the prayer which is why God instructs for a private meeting with Him.

How does God answer our prayer? God's answer is through His Spirit, the very omnipresence of His power. Nothing is created without the power of God. It was God as the Word who fashioned the heavens and the earth. God spoke His Word and the Holy Spirit manifested.

When God designed man of His Spirit, He presented Himself as Christ and as the Holy Spirit that He would always be with His children. God has never left His people, not the Israelites, nor the Gentiles in the four-thousand years depicted in the Old Testament, nor the remaining two-thousand years in the New Testament since Christ. We are the generation living in the remaining years of the six-thousandth year since the foundation, and God is still with His children. If you are not aware of what has been given to you in Christ and in the Holy Spirit, then you will remain without the promises that God provided when He created man.

What does God say? We are instructed to know what God has done on our behalf, what He gives and how He administers His blessings to His children. One of the obstacles to receiving is our *lack of knowledge* which leaves us void of His promises. *My people are destroyed for lack of knowledge: because thou hast rejected knowledge, I will also reject thee.* Hosea 4:6

This verse is in the Old Testament when the Israelites rejected God as their King. They whined and complained about everything, but never praised Him as the God who took them out of bondage, loved them, and had a homeland prepared for them. They were a prideful people who didn't understand the love of God.

Today, we are still a prideful people who complain and accuse when God doesn't come forth with our desires. Just like the Israelites who refused God, we blame Him for our shortcomings. We hold Him hostage with our unbelief and assault Him with accusations of withholding His power when our prayer isn't answered.

As a people, we have failed miserably in our understanding God which has hampered an intimate relationship with Him. This is evident throughout the generations since Adam in the Garden of Eden, for we continue to be prodigal children. Even with God giving us a birth in His Spirit, we have not turned away from our old carnal self and accept the Spirit of God. We wander aimlessly searching for God, wanting His power, and in desperate need of His intervention not realizing He has been with us all along, never forgotten. In fact, so close, we don't see Him, nor feel His presence, never forsaken.

What has happened? We continue to reject rather than accept. We hold to the old, rather than seek the new; meaning, we are still living under the law of Moses, rather in the grace given by Jesus Christ. We admire biblical history as entertaining stories, but don't acknowledge the reality that God is exemplifying His Word through the lives of generations past. We are more comfortable with the proclamation of man's gospel than speaking with God personally, and then we wonder why we aren't receiving His blessings. We are modern day Israelites.

As a believer in the Son of God, we know Christ died on the Cross for our sins, and we agree salvation is eternal, but what does this mean in terms of God's promises? You are born of the Spirit of God and you are given the power of God, the Holy Spirit, who lives in your heart. Your natural body is now the temple of God. *What? know ye not that <u>your body is the temple of the Holy Ghost which is in you</u>, which ye have of God, and ye are not your own?* 1 Corinthians 6:9

Simply stated, you have the power of God in you. The Holy Spirit responds to the person professing in prayer and supplication. In the Old Testament era before Christ, the Holy Spirit came upon someone and left. They did not have the Holy Spirit within them. Christ was the only person to have the Holy Spirit; and thus, could heal and perform miracles. Upon Jesus' baptism in Jordan, the Holy Spirit descended from the Kingdom of Heaven as a dove. *Behold my servant, whom I have chosen; my beloved, in whom my soul is well pleased: I will put my spirit upon him, and he shall show judgment to the Gentiles.* Matthew 12:18

When Jesus returned to the throne, He gave another Comforter to His disciples, for He explained He would no longer be with them but would send someone in His place. They weren't able to receive the Spirit of Christ after His crucifixion but were empowered with the Holy Spirit to continue His ministry. *And I will ask the Father, and He shall give you another Comforter, that he may abide with you for ever; Even the <u>Spirit of truth</u>; whom the world cannot receive, because it seeth him not, neither knoweth him: but ye know him; for he dwelleth with you, and shall be in you.* John 14:16-17 We know this was fifty days after His resurrection, the Day of Pentecost in the Upper Room in Jerusalem. As God placed His Spirit in His Son, and Christ sent the Holy Spirit to His disciples, so is the gift of the Holy Spirit given to you when you are born into the Kingdom of Heaven.

You now possess the Spirit of Christ and the power of the Holy Spirit. You are a new creation born of Spirit into God's spiritual Kingdom. At the birth of your spirit person, the first responsibility is to pray to the Father that you acknowledge His gift by asking for the Holy Spirit to be quickened, or awakened. The Holy Spirit, who is God, performs many functions in our life. The first is to teach about the Kingdom principles.

Unfortunately, many have not been taught about the Holy Spirit and are without His power; thus, it would be a challenge to have a prayer answered when the source hasn't been acknowledged. God is always providing to His children, but our carnal efforts will not release supernatural power. God has set forth the method to come before Him. It must always be your *spirit person* through the *Holy Spirit* to the *Spirit of God* to enter His *spiritual* Kingdom.

This is a key factor in prayers being answered. The Holy Spirit must be a participant to receive the blessings, gifts, and all the promises of the Father. Jesus performed no miracles or healing until He was baptized with the Holy Spirit, and it is the same for us today. We must also be baptized with the Holy Spirit that the power of the Kingdom of Heaven comes to Earth on our behalf.

This remains a reason why believers are without answered prayers. Here is a true story. A young couple's first child was born with an unknown condition that had doctors baffled and because they had no remedy, they pronounced the infant had a very short time to live. Being a couple of faith, they went to their pastor and asked that he and the elders of the church pray for their baby girl. They obliged and were so certain the child was healed, the pastor made a proclamation to the congregation that God had healed the baby. Within the week, the infant died. The following Sunday morning, the pastor made another announcement to the congregation and his words were: *I don't know why God didn't heal the baby, I was so sure he had, but it must have been His will that she not live.*

People accept this belief about God, but it is not His truth. God isn't taking your loved ones from you, ever. As long as you choose to believe a false perception, why would you expect Him to give you answered prayers when you believe it is His will to place harm in your life? God is a sovereign King; however, He is not dispensing ill-will upon you for any reason but rather grace flows whereby all His blessings are supplied. This is a perfect example of living under the law whereby wrath is dispensed rather than accepting all that Christ gave upon His death on the Cross.

There are factors in this story as to why the baby wasn't healed but the most prevalent is the lack of God's power through the Holy Spirit. It seems apparent that Kingdom supernatural power wasn't operating among anyone praying for this infant.

Another incident of prayers that were answered. A young couple whose baby boy was born with a heart condition and would eventually need open heart surgery. They also brought many to pray over their baby along with their own ongoing diligent prayers for three years, and yet, no answer was forthcoming. They didn't understand why God had not healed their son's heart. However, once they realized and accepted that it was God's will to heal and that God had not given them a child with a defective heart, they opened themselves to the truth of His Word.

They learned that what they believed was actually grounded in unbelief which restricted the power of God. The *lack of receiving was within their belief,* and they repented of their unbelief and accepted God's truth, whereby the one fervent prayer held in faith gave them the answer they sought. The young couple learned how to pray appropriately in belief and the power of God flowed through the Holy Spirit rendering their miracle. The next medical report taken on their son showed a perfect heart.

There are numerous stories of individuals healed of cancer; one report they have it and the next there is no evidence. What is the variance in these stories? The power of God released through the Holy Spirit to those who trust with unwavering faith. The truth in these stories is God never withholds His power from flowing into our life; however, we restrict the flow by what we believe. Anything other than believing He is always providing through what His Son did on the Cross is a restriction placing us in an unbelief status and will always negate belief. As believers, we think our faith is steadfast; however, if our faith isn't rendering results this is the moment to reevaluate for unbelief. Unbelief can manifest in many ways, and typically, unknowingly.

Therefore, acknowledge that God does not withhold from His children. His promises are in place and released by living according to the principles of His Kingdom. Prayers are answered by aligning our belief according to His Word, so the answer is forthcoming. When praying for a situation and finding you aren't hearing from the Father, this is the juncture to seriously review what you hold to be your truth. Believing a false gospel presents unbelief which will void receiving an answer. The Holy Spirit, the very essence of Kingdom power, will not respond to erroneous belief.

The authority to approach the throne is in the Son, and the power flows through the Holy Spirit. *For the prophecy came not in old time by the will of man: but holy men of God spake as they were moved by the Holy Ghost.* 2 Peter 1:21 The Holy Spirit is with you at all times; therefore, God is always supplying. His blessings are within you because you have the provider of those gifts within you. Otherwise, how can a supernatural gift be given in your natural circumstance without an avenue to make it possible? Your Kingdom provision is within you!

Many doctrines do not teach of the Holy Spirit, so it renders pause in the first story to strongly consider that the Holy Spirit wasn't present in either the young couple nor the church affiliates, for if He was, there would have been a different outcome. Healing and miracles are gifts and the Holy Spirit does not withhold to those who seek Him in truth.

You can be a believer in Christ and have unbelief. Recall the disciples had an incident when they were unable to remove a demon spirit and asked Jesus privately why they could not. He answered and told them it was because of their unbelief. Though it may seem an oxymoron, but unbelief is prevalent in the believers realm. Many Christians profess their belief, not realizing unbelief is present. Unbelief negates anything that belief provides.

The Law versus Grace

In the Old Testament era when people were under the law, it was the priest they went to because he was the representative of God for the removal of sins. We have a tendency today to maintain an *under the law* mentality which will not provide Kingdom promises because we are no longer under the law but live in grace given by Christ. *For the law was given by Moses, but grace and truth came by Jesus Christ.* John 1:17 The law was fulfilled in Christ on the Cross and grace is the outflow. The law, the Ten Commandments, administered by Moses to the Israelites existed for a short period of time, only fifteen-hundred years from Moses to Christ. It is noteworthy that Adam, Noah, and Abraham (before Moses) were not under the law.

Though God had a covenant with each, it is Moses and Christ who represent the mediators of God's Word. Moses, a servant of God and Christ, the Son of God. Under the law, we witness the anger of God towards His wayward people; however, in Christ we receive His blessings. Under the law, the people were continuously disobedient, whereby in Christ we live in obedience through grace. We are born righteous in Christ and this is how the Father sees His children.

It is no longer mandatory to go to a priest, pastor, or anyone else for forgiveness of sins, healing, a miracle, or anything required of God. The veil which separated God from man was ripped down the middle upon Jesus' death on the Cross. *And, behold, the veil of the temple was rent in twain from the top to the bottom; and the earth did quake, and the rocks rent.* Matthew 27:51 We are now intimately connected to God through His Son; therefore, there is no longer a physical temple with a priest. The middle spokesperson between God and man has been removed in our new covenant in Christ.

It is a misguided approach to go to another when God tells us to come to Him, personally. It would be like your child needing to ask something of you, but he sends a friend to ask in his place. Wouldn't you want to hear directly from your own child? This is what our heavenly Father is saying: *come to me, I already know what you will ask, but I want to hear it directly from you, my beloved child.*

When we come to the Father personally, we do so because of what the Son has given, not man. If you approach God under the law and not by the grace given in His Son, this becomes a crucial problem. Should your belief be in the law, then you remain under the law which depicts the wrath of God. God's anger towards the Israelites was because of their unbelief and refusal to accept Him as their King. In the New Testament, Christ fulfilled the law on the Cross. Grace is where the blessings and promises of God flow because God sees His children through His Son's righteousness. There is no wrath in grace.

Many Christians continue to remain in an *under the law* mentality that God gives diseases and hardship to teach a lesson, to bring the individual closer to Him. If this were true, why pray for Him to remove the very thing you believe He wants you to have? If you believe God has given you a disease, why go to a doctor for a cure when God wants you to suffer to learn a lesson?

This belief is so convoluted with a false doctrine that a person can literally drown in the atrocity of it. Should your traditional teachings encourage this *under the law* belief, don't expect prayers to be answered because you are grossly believing wrong of God. More so, you are not acknowledging the measure of the sacrifice of His Son. *I do not frustrate the grace of God: for if righteousness come by the law, then Christ is dead in vain.* Galatians 2:21 There is no righteousness in the law. Righteousness is the Son, whereby sin is no longer an issue with God.

When grace was given by Christ at the Cross, the law was fulfilled. Grace supplies God's blessings, but the law prevents anything of God from ever reaching you. Blessings do not come forth from the law. There were no blessings under the law for the Israelites. *And the Levites shall speak, and say unto all the men of Israel with a loud voice, Cursed be the man that maketh any graven or molten image, an abomination unto the Lord, the work of the hands of the craftsman, and putteth it in a secret place. And all the people shall answer and say, Amen. Cursed be he that setteth light by his father or his mother. And all the people shall say, Amen. Cursed be he that removeth his neighbour's landmark. And all the people shall say, Amen. Cursed be he that maketh the blind to wander out of the way. And all the people shall say, Amen. Cursed be he that perverteth the judgment of the stranger, fatherless, and widow. And all the people shall say, Amen. Cursed be he that lieth with his father's wife; because he uncovereth his father's skirt. And all the people shall say, Amen. Cursed be he that lieth with any manner of beast. And all the people shall say, Amen. Cursed be he that lieth with his sister, the daughter of his father, or the daughter of his mother. And all the people shall say, Amen. Cursed be he that lieth with his mother in law. And all the people shall say, Amen. Cursed be he that smiteth his neighbour secretly. And all the people shall say, Amen. Cursed be he that taketh reward to slay an innocent person. And all the people shall say, Amen. Cursed be he that confirmeth not all the words of this law to do them. And all the people shall say, Amen.* Deuteronomy 27:14-26 Notice how when the law was administered, the people agreed to curses with an Amen, but there where no blessings mentioned, or given. This exemplifies the self-righteousness of the Israelites and their arrogance that whatever was put before them they could do.

If your faith is based *under the law* and you believe God is dispensing wrath in your life, then that is exactly what you'll have, what the law gives. *Because the <u>law</u>*

worketh wrath: for where no law is, there is no transgression. Romans 4:15 Judgement is in wrath; however, in Christ, we are no longer under judgement. If your belief is of the servant and not the Son, you have missed living in the foundation of grace. Anything other than accepting the finished work of the Son for the Father is a rejection of Christ's death on the Cross.

Accepting your position of righteousness as given in your spirit birth in Christ, you will receive blessings. *I do not frustrate the grace of God: for if righteousness come by the law, then Christ is dead in vain.* Galatians 2:21 Our righteousness is solely through Jesus Christ. It is about what you believe which determines what you receive from the Kingdom. It is not God withholding, but you restricting the supernatural power based on your belief.

In Christ, we take a position of rest which means we don't allow our instinctive nature, our human efforts to control the matter as though God needs our help. What is required is to rest in faith and trust that what is asked will be given. *Let us labour therefore to enter into that rest, lest any man fall after the same example of unbelief.* Hebrews 4:11 Don't try to fix the problem once you have turned it over to God, for if you do, then you have shown unbelief.

If you are trying to find a solution and expect God to do the same, it's a wash. Your efforts just voided God's resolution. How? You aren't trusting (rest) in His Word. That is why He says we labour to rest. It's a struggle to do nothing and wait on the Lord to do everything. Rest is a position of faith, of trust, of acknowledging He has taken care of the matter. Wait for Him to supply your answer which He lovingly provides through grace. The Father delights in giving to His children; therefore, be cautious to not hinder the flow of His blessings.

Kingdom Principles

The principles which govern God's Kingdom were established at the foundation. There is order and laws just as the natural laws of our earthen life. When God was establishing His Kingdom, what was His desire? His plan was to fill the Kingdom with children, for everything was made for us. *Fear not, little flock; for it is your Father's good pleasure to give you the kingdom.* Luke 12:32 He is an Almighty King but also desires to be a Father, and it pleases Him to give His children a place in His home, mansions prepared for our eternal life.

We are born of Adam's corruptible seed becoming prodigal children (sin); however, the second Adam, Christ, removed the sin and birthed us incorruptible (righteous) which allows us to live in the Father's home upon our asking to be born into His Kingdom. This occurs today, spiritually, and remains for eternity.

The Father is pleased to see His home filled with children that He declares: *I will give you the keys of the kingdom of heaven; and whatever you bind on earth shall have been bound in heaven, and whatever you loose on earth shall have been loosed in heaven.* Matthew 16:19 This is a very strong proclamation from God. Did you catch what God just said? His Kingdom is open to you and all the treasures in His home are for you right now; therefore, what you require in your earthen life is supplied, nothing withheld.

The question is what does it mean bound on earth,

or loosed on earth will also reflect the same in Heaven? Literally speaking, our Father has given His children the key to receive all that He has prepared. This is a perfect example that God does not withhold from His children. Since the Kingdom key has been given to you, it behooves you to know what the key is and how to apply it within the Kingdom to receive.

Kingdom power is always available because the supernatural power is within you, the Holy Spirit. It is the Spirit of God who supplies when we ask with a believing heart and maintain trust in our thoughts. The Holy Spirit provides the promises of God when we live according to the Spirit. Though we have the key to the Kingdom (Holy Spirit), we can block His power working on our behalf.

Therefore, we have the ability to block, or loose on Earth and in Heaven, simultaneously, the power of God. We can literally prevent the supernatural power from entering our life even though we have the Spirit of God within us. How do we do this? Unbelief, holding onto a false teaching of God. Power is not activated under a false belief. Only the truth by the Spirit of Truth will answer a prayer. We sabotage ourselves with the lack of Kingdom knowledge.

We want to dictate how we pray and then wonder why it doesn't work. We may think that we can put the parts of a bicycle together because we've ridden one in our lifetime. However, in attempting to do so without the instruction manual, we find ourself failing at the task. We need the manual to instruct on how to put it together correctly.

Praying to the Father without an intimate relationship with Him surely hampers what we may expect to receive. He wants His children to speak with Him about their concerns, but our carnal nature often gets in the way, especially when we adopt a false concept of God.

Righteous Living in Christ

There are many things that can block receiving from God. We aren't perfect, but there are responsibilities in our righteous position in Christ. Sin is no longer an issue with God; however, choosing to remain with a sinful nature can prohibit receiving from the Kingdom of Heaven. For example, holding onto anger or bitterness toward someone. *But if ye forgive not men their trespasses, neither will your Father forgive your trespasses.* Matthew 6:15 Is this blocking the Father's response? Have you unknowingly stepped out of grace? Something to consider.

If your child has been disobedient, you aren't likely to reward him/her with an elaborate gift. It's always the Father's desire to give to His children, for He delights in giving because He loves you, but is your behavior that of an ungrateful child?

This is not about trying to be a perfect person, for only One person on Earth was perfect and that is Christ, the Son of God. However, we should live as a righteous person because of the gift of righteousness. As we are joint-heirs in Christ within the Kingdom and seated with Him, spiritually, there should be no excuse for not having the wisdom to obtain blessings for our earthen life.

For example, you aren't going to obtain a private meeting with the judge in a case you are pleading in court. You'll need a spokesperson to speak on your behalf and typically this is an attorney, someone acceptable to the courtroom who understands the rules and regulations that govern how you may present your case. The same holds true in the Kingdom. You can only receive of the Kingdom through a spirit mediator who is your advocate and stands before your Almighty King and lets your request be known.

Just as a judge knows the details of the case before it is presented in his courtroom, so does our King know of the reasons you come before Him in prayer. Therefore, your prayers must be submitted through the means that God established. Our carnal attempt and on Christ's name will not release a response. Why? Because it is our intercessor, the Holy Spirit, who dispenses the treasures we seek upon our faithfulness. Christ's name gives us the authority to ask the Holy Spirit to move on our behalf.

Likened to an analogy of an office environment: when we submit our purchase order (prayer) for a specific supply request, it is the Holy Spirit who knows how to correct the requisition (prayer) and fulfill the order (answered prayer) on behalf of the Father. *Likewise the Spirit also helpeth our infirmities: for <u>we know not what we should pray for as we ought</u>: but the <u>Spirit itself maketh intercession for us</u> with groanings which cannot be uttered.* Romans 8:26

With your complete reliance on the Holy Spirit, there should be no unbelief (doubt) that you will receive. The Father is supplying through the Holy Spirit who is always <u>with you</u>, for He is <u>in you</u>. Therefore, never doubt God's provision, for all things are given to the righteous child born of the Spirit of Christ.

Faith versus Faith

There are two types of faith. One faith is the faith of the believer, meaning our faith in God and His Son for salvation. This is the faith we hold onto in our trust in Him which is an <u>action</u> on our part to believe and have faith in the knowledge of the Kingdom.

However, the second faith is <u>given</u> as a gift. This faith comes from the Holy Spirit, one of His nine gifts for man's earthen life. The Holy Spirit gives His faith when our faith is present. This gives clarity to the importance that unbelief can show up in many forms. Our faith with the Holy Spirit's faith match like a key to a lock to release the storehouse of treasures within the Kingdom of Heaven. The faith which is a gift of the Holy Spirit is the faith God provides.

Our faith is measured in the equivalence of a mustard seed. *And Jesus said unto them, Because of your unbelief: for verily I say unto you, If ye have faith as a grain of mustard seed, ye shall say unto this mountain, Remove hence to yonder place; and it shall remove; and nothing shall be impossible unto you.* Matthew 17:20 The disciples were given the ability to perform the same miracles that Jesus did, for He gave them the Holy Spirit. However, as human beings susceptible to carnal thoughts, they fell short in their belief, for they could not remove a demon from a child.

These gifts are how the power of God is given. *Now there are diversities of gifts, but the same Spirit. And there are differences of administrations, but the same Lord. And there are diversities of operations, but it is the same God which worketh all in all. But the manifestation* *of the Spirit is given to every man to profit withal. For to one is given by the Spirit the word of **wisdom**; to another the word of **knowledge** by the same Spirit; To another **faith** by the same Spirit; to another the gifts of **healing** by the same Spirit; To another the working of **miracles**; to another **prophecy**; to another **discerning of spirits**; to another **divers kinds of tongues**; to another the **interpretation of tongues**: But all these worketh that one and the selfsame Spirit, dividing to every man severally as he will.* 1 Corinthians 12:4-11

Notice nothing is lacking in the arsenal needed to live as a spirit person when we have the active presence of the Holy Spirit. Pray that the gift of faith from the Holy Spirit strengthens your faith to receive. *And straightway the father of the child cried out, and said with tears, Lord, I believe; help thou mine unbelief.* Mark 9:24

There is a purpose for Christ and a purpose for the Holy Spirit, both being God. God requires we know what each provides. When we seek God in prayer and there is no response, don't take the mindset that God isn't going to help. This is never His truth. The reality is that we don't have the truth, though we may think we do.

God is Never at Fault

When it comes to understanding God's nature, many believers take a simpleminded approach and accuse our Almighty King of withholding His greatness. Like a child performing a temper-tantrum, whining over what is perceived an injustice. It is much easier to blame the One who should be supplying rather than the one who is asking. Lack of Kingdom precepts is prevalent among Christians, and yet, we don't see where the problem lies.

Filing a complaint to the King about the King's behavior is foolish. Meaning, holding God ransom with a false belief system and accusing Him of not answering your prayer would be unforgivable before a judge. Because our Father loves His children, He overlooks our tantrum; however, we have inhibited His blessings. As His children, we should know better than to accuse our Father, yet we do it anyway. Perhaps, it soothes our hurt feelings and lessens our burden for not understanding.

Instead of pointing a finger at God, we should take a deeper look within ourselves for what we may be missing in knowledge of the Father's Word. Even when we believe we have done everything right, prayed the right way, believed on His Word, held our faith, and trusted He would come through but when we see no evidence, we don't understand why.

We turn away from Him instead drawing closer with a heartfelt desire for His truth. God does not pull away from His children. *The Lord is good, a <u>strong hold in the day of trouble</u>; and he knoweth them that <u>trust in him</u>.* Nahum 1:7 We have missed the gift of knowledge from the Spirit of Truth. Once again, we witness the necessity of our dependency on the Holy Spirit and His gifts.

God is steadfast, for we are never forgotten or forsaken, His position never changes. God is love and we are forever deeply loved. *He that loveth not, knoweth not God, for God is love.* 1 John 4:8 With an all encompassing agape love for you, it is impossible for God to withhold His blessings in your life.

There is nothing that God will need to add, change, alter, correct, or withhold for any reason. Knowing that

God has prepared for our lives, planned our destiny, knows every hair on our head, and knows what we will come to Him in prayer before we utter the first word, then surely we are the ones amiss.

This is where we must learn His Word and know how to approach the throne of God. *Receive my <u>instructions</u>, and not silver; and <u>knowledge</u> rather than choice gold.* Proverbs 8:10 Also, He tells us: *Apply thine heart unto <u>instruction</u>, and thine ears to the words of <u>knowledge</u>.* Proverbs 23:12 God is instructing us to educate ourselves in spiritual wisdom, the wisdom that comes from the Holy Spirit, that we may learn how to live within His Spirit Kingdom.

Our approach must be in the spirit. It is our spirit person on the <u>authority</u> in Christ and through the <u>provision</u> of the Holy Spirit that we may receive of the Kingdom of Heaven which is a spirit realm. Prayers are answered in the Spirit realm and manifested in the earthen realm on our behalf.

Living in the Spirit Realm

We know that God is the Father, the Son, and the Holy Spirit. God presented Himself to the Israelites as Himself at Mount Sinai when He came down in the cloud and spoke to them after removing them from bondage in Egypt. In the era that God was dealing with the Israelites, He communicated with them through appointed people, or prophets. They did not have Christ and the Holy Spirit. However, Christ was exemplified throughout the Old Testament before He was born of flesh and became man's reality.

It is in these past two-thousand years since Christ, we have been given a new mediator, a covenant in Christ. *This is the covenant that I will make with them after those days, saith the Lord, I will put my laws into their hearts, and in their minds will I write them; and their sins and iniquities I will remember no more.* Hebrews 10:16-17

One of the precepts is that we must *ask* for anything we need of God (note: this is not referring to materialistic possessions but receiving spirit gifts from the spirit Kingdom for our spirit person). He does not arbitrarily throw gifts down to His children. They are administered by the Holy Spirit who discerns which gift is applicable for our need. As we are required to ask to be born into the spirit realm (free will), this should be our first clue that we must also ask for His promises of blessings, gifts, and supernatural power that has been established for us....*for the asking*.

As a child, surely you remember your parents teaching you to say *please* when you asked for something. Likewise, our heavenly Father requires that when we ask of Him, we do so in the manner He tells us and with much thanksgiving. *Be careful for nothing; but in every thing by prayer and supplication with <u>thanksgiving let your requests be made known unto God</u>.* Philippians 5:6 God has just told us how to properly approach Him in prayer. We do so with much thanksgiving; thanking Him that what we have requested has already been given. Any other method of praying shows a lack of trust that He will supply, unbelief.

There is a methodical or orderly manner to entering into God's Kingdom. Just as there are natural laws we must obey in our earthen life such as paying taxes, stopping at red lights, and so forth, there are also laws within the Kingdom. There is precision in God's work. Our Father takes care of His children while we remain in this earthen world. This is why the Holy Spirit is with us and we should call upon Him.

Though we remain surrounded by corruption in this world, once cleansed from the sin nature in Christ, our goal is to live spiritually. *Therefore we are buried with him by baptism into death: that like as Christ was raised up from the dead by the glory of the Father, even so we also should <u>walk in newness of life</u>.* Romans 6:4 We are born into the spirit realm of God and made a new creation for the Kingdom. *Therefore if any man be in Christ, he is a new creature: old things are passed away, behold, all things are become new.* 2 Corinthians 5:17

Our spirit birth is fresh, untouched of sin; a newborn birthed in the Spirit of Christ for the parent, God. Take a moment and meditate on the awesomeness of what has just transpired in the Kingdom as angels sing upon the spiritual birth of a child. *Likewise, I say unto you, there is joy in the presence of the angels of God over one sinner that repenteth.* Luke 15:10

Just as the natural birth of a baby brings forth gifts from family and friends, and as the wise men brought precious gifts to the newborn King, so your heavenly Father has gifts for you, His precious child. There isn't anything He will not do for you. Just as you protect and provide for your children, so much more does God love, protect, and provide for His own.

Many fail to realize the significance of a birth into the Kingdom. We can only receive the treasures within the Kingdom through the Holy Spirit on the authority in Christ. Our soul and body is not capable of achieving this, and yet, we rely on our human skills to attempt entrance into the Kingdom. *Because the <u>carnal mind is enmity against God</u>: for it is not subject to the law of God, neither indeed can be. So then they that are in the flesh cannot please God.* Romans 8:7-8 Continuing to rely on our carnal nature, our human thought, rather than our spirit person who has a direct relationship with the Father will leave us empty-handed.

We cannot live with one foot grounded in the desires of the earthen life and one foot expecting heavenly treasures at the same time. The carnal mind is enmity against God; and therefore, cannot enter into the Kingdom because of the corruptibility of man just as Adam could not remain in the Garden once sin came upon him. Even though born righteous in Christ, as long as we remain in this corruptible world, there is the ability to be tainted. Therefore, attempting to pray with carnal thought places a block to receiving answers. God is Spirit, so we must pray in the spirit.

God hears our prayers and is deeply saddened to see our pain, sorrow, and suffering whether emotional or physical. However, He cannot change the precepts that He set at the foundation. Laws are in place and must be followed. *And be not <u>conformed to this world</u>: but be ye <u>transformed by the renewing of your mind</u> that ye may prove what is that good, and acceptable, and perfect will of God.* Romans 12:2 Everything God has done is for man, and we are responsible for our relationship with Him.

Just as God gives man a *free will* to choose between a life of sin or a sinless life through a rebirth in Christ, we should use our free will to live as a spirit person. *It is sown a natural body; it is raised a spiritual body. There is a natural body, and there is a spiritual body.* 1 Corinthians 15:44 Always maintain emphasis on your spirit person and mature in knowledge and wisdom of God's Word and live a bountiful life with the blessings He so desires to bestow upon you.

Consider this analogy. Traveling to a foreign country without some knowledge and ability to speak their native language will make it difficult to convey your request for ordering a meal, making a purchase, or for any accommodations. This holds true in living a spirit life to receive blessings, gifts, and supernatural power.

Knowing God is Spirit, it can only be in the spirit that we pray through the Holy Spirit to receive the gifts from the Father. Your *spirit*, through the *Holy Spirit* for the *Spirit of God,* for all blessings of the Father are of the Spirit. And all gifts of the Spirit of God are administered through the Spirit of Truth. Praying with carnal thought is enmity against God because we can still be tainted by the things that block the Spirit of Truth.

Summary of a Fervent Prayer

*Likewise the Spirit also helpeth our infirmities:
for we know not what we should pray for as
we ought: but the Spirit itself maketh intercession
for us with groanings which cannot be uttered.*
Romans 8:26

In summary, the first requirement is to be born of the spirit in Christ and receive His gift of the Holy Spirit. Pray that the Holy Spirit be an active participant in your life and learn to depend on Him. God is the Holy Spirit and His power comes through the third person of the Trinity of God. He is your advocate in the Kingdom, your protector and provider and with you at all times.

It is crucial to not live under the dictates of the old law but be mindful to live in the grace that Christ has given. God isn't dispensing wrath to His children, but is supplying blessings through grace, for He sees you righteous through His Son; therefore, the Father sees no sin in you.

Take note of the things in your life that may be a hinderance, or blocking the flow of blessings reaching you. Rebuke all the negatives and expect blessings.

Accept there are two types of faith, so that you hold strong in your action of the faith of a mustard seed as the Spirit of Truth provides the supernatural faith to supply what you desire.

Know that all blessings, promises, and gifts are freely given for the asking; however, ask as a believer, not in doubt (unbelief) wondering if God may or may not provide. Hold steadfast that what you have spoken to your heavenly Father has already been supplied and maintain faith as you wait for the manifestation in your natural life.

Pray with praise and thanksgiving always giving the glory to your Almighty King, for it pleases Him to hear you are thankful of His gifts. Accept how deeply you are loved and how precious you are to the Father, for you are born of His Son.

A MARRIAGE GIFT

Wherefore, my brethren, ye also are become dead to the law by the body of Christ; that ye should be married to another, even to him who is raised from the dead, that we should bring forth fruit unto God.
Romans 1:4

Let's step back to the basics for a moment. We are born a physical person into a natural world. We grew up understanding the laws, or rules of how to live in society; what is acceptable conduct. We have a soul, our thoughts, which determines our personality and behavior and is influenced by the natural senses of what we see, hear, taste, touch, and smell. Now add an emotion such as happiness, sadness, anger, hurt, confusion, depression, laughter, fear, and so forth. This becomes the constitution of our natural life.

When combining the physical senses with emotions, we are capable of making human decisions and choices. We completely understand this because we have been taught from birth. This is our natural life and normal to who we are as a person.

However, there is a third part of man and that is the spirit, for we are the trinity of body, soul, and spirit. We know the body and soul respond to the natural elements and there is a spirit within that can only be awakened through a birth in Christ. Until such time we choose to be born into the Kingdom of Heaven, the spirit cannot be called upon to perform any function in our daily life. Our spirit person is for a relationship with God and meant for eternity; therefore, our spirit only responds to the spirit realm.

Upon our rebirth, the body becomes the temple for the Holy Spirit; and thus, it should be our spirit guided by the Holy Spirit in command of our soul and body. *What? Know ye not that your body is the temple of the Holy Ghost which is in you, which ye have of God, and ye are not your own?* 1 Corinthians 6:19

As we mature in God's Word, our spirit person grows in knowledge and wisdom taught by the *Spirit of Truth*, so that the decisions we make are directed by our spirit and not our soul. At all times be mindful of the spiritual realm of God and not be influenced by the earthen.

There are two worlds to consider; the natural and the spirit. As stated, born into the natural, the earthen, is understood but born into the spirit must be learned. *That which is born of the flesh is flesh; and that which is born of the Spirit is spirit.* John 3:6 It's easy to accept the natural world; however, when choosing God, we acknowledge His spiritual Kingdom.

The Father has a gift for each of His children, one that enables us to have a relationship with Him, a continuous fellowship and communion. The gift of the Holy Spirit brings all things of God into our life, for the Holy Spirit is God. *Now we have received, not the spirit of the world, but the spirit which is God; that we might know the things that are freely given to us of God.* 1 Corinthians 2:12 Do we truly acknowledge the magnitude of His presence? Unfortunately, most do not.

The Marriage Covenant

It is at this juncture that many remain lost to the blessings from the Father because they don't know they have a responsibility to a covenant made in Christ when they asked to be born into the Kingdom. You may have thought your birth was solely for salvation, and if so, then you've missed the magnificence of your spirit birth. You agreed to a marriage in Christ for the Father when you accepted Christ as your Lord. Not marrying God, but a commitment to Him in Christ.

This is why when Christ returns for the saints, His bride, there will be a marriage supper in the Kingdom of Heaven for the *official* joining of the children to the King. *And he saith unto me, write, blessed are they which are called unto the marriage supper of the Lamb. And he saith unto me, These are the true sayings of God.* Revelation 19:9

Before Christ's death on the Cross, His resurrection and ascension back to the throne in the Kingdom, there was the ceremonial last supper, the *Lord's Supper,* with His chosen disciples. Upon His return, He will take His bride to His Kingdom and there will be a ceremonial marriage supper. Christ has made you a joint-heir in the Kingdom of Heaven because you are married to Him and with Him, spiritually.

This covenant is not an insignificant matter, but an eternal commitment. Just as in marriage to another person, you take vows to love, honor, and cherish one another, it is the same in your decision to be born in Christ. The initial gift of exchanging rings is symbolic of the bond and commitment to each other.

As God has established the husband as head of the wife, he is to love her as God loves His church (children). This is not a reference that the wife is subservient to the husband, but rather an instruction from God telling man that for as much as He (God) loves His children and cares for their needs, so is the husband to do the same.

He is to protect, provide, and love her forever; *until death do us part*. Also, what the husband owns, she has entitlement of joint-ownership. In this analogy, we can see the parallel of the components love, protect, and provide defining a natural marriage are the very same in our commitment to God, for God loves, protects, and provides with the gift of the Holy Spirit that binds us to Him. As a comparison, it could be said that the Holy Spirit is our symbolic ring; however, there is much, much more to having the Holy Spirit in our life.

Everything the Father has within His home (Kingdom) now belongs to His children. *For the Lord God is a sun and shield: the Lord will give grace and glory: no good thing will he withhold from them that walk uprightly.* Psalm 84:11 As a new creation in Christ, a newborn spirit person, we are prepared to live righteously, to *walk uprightly, and to* live by the Kingdom precepts from the Father.

If unaware of the significance of what transpired, we can blindly block our relationship with God. Because of our human inclination and influence of this earthen world, we neglect to rely on our Kingdom intercessor. *Likewise the Spirit also helpeth our infirmities: for we know not what we should pray for as we ought: but the Spirit itself maketh intercession for us with groanings which cannot be uttered.* Romans 8:26 The Holy Spirit, the Spirit of Truth, is our provider.

Our prayer is to show the Father our trust. *He therefore that despiseth, despiseth not man, but God, who hath also <u>given unto us his Holy Spirit</u>.* 1 Timothy 4:8 An answer to a prayer is within you because the power of God is within you. *Who hath also <u>sealed us</u>, and given the earnest of the <u>Spirit in our hearts</u>.* 2 Corinthians 1:22 Here is our answer to receiving blessings, promises, and gifts from the Father. *The blessing of the Lord, it maketh rich, and he addeth no sorrow with it.* Proverbs 10:22 God deeply desires for a relationship with His children. It truly is unimaginable that anyone would not want this intimate communion with their heavenly Father.

Our fellowship with God begins with our desire to have a relationship with Him, to learn of His love, to accept His Kingdom principles, and to allow the Holy Spirit to teach all things of the Father. *For they that are after the flesh do mind the things of the flesh; but they that are after the Spirit the things of the Spirit.* Romans 8:5 Our spirit is *alive* waiting for instructions, eager to grow in wisdom of the Father's Word.

The Marriage Gift

Our spirit knows the Holy Spirit is in our heart, but if our soul keeps Him at a distance and never allows communication with Him, then our spirit person doesn't have an opportunity to mature; and unfortunately, remains an infant without Kingdom wisdom. Don't find yourself disconnected wandering aimlessly without the guidance of the Spirit of Truth. This can easily happen if not grounded in God's Word.

The Father's treasures are literally at our disposal, so that His spiritual gifts may be given when we ask. Blessings of the Father are _gifts_ and that which we desire must be _asked_. God is not going to randomly throw gifts into our life; however, we ask according to His instructions.

The responsibility in receiving spiritual gifts is in diligently learning to live spiritually. This is why carnal prayers do not render an answer. *Which things also we speak, not in the words which man's wisdom teacheth, but which the Holy Ghost teacheth; comparing spiritual things with spiritual.* 1 Corinthians 2:13 Mindful of our ability to be corrupted and with an instinctive nature towards self-righteousness, we can easily fail in this area of our relationship with our Father. One main reason is that in our carnal nature, we would be remiss to give Him the thanksgiving, glory, and praise. This is the position most required in our prayers; glorifying God and being thankful for the blessings.

It appears evident that mainstream doctrines lack in teaching of the Holy Spirit. If they did, there would be more believers receiving answered prayers which raises the question: Why are they not helping Christians to learn of the Trinity of God; and thus, the precepts that govern His Kingdom? Perhaps, because they never learned for themselves; after all, you can't teach something you don't know. *Beware lest any man spoil you through philosophy and vain deceit, after the tradition of men, after the rudiments of the world, and not after Christ.* Colossians 2:8

Man passes traditions and doctrines down through generations and holds them as truth. Teaching of the Holy Spirit is blindly withheld, or purposefully glazed over in congregations because of a lack of knowledge in the very individuals professing the word of God. It is the greatest deception embedded within denominations that specifically prevents the knowledge of the *power* that is within each child of the Father.

We listen to the teachings of man and not God. *Making the word of God of none effect through your tradition, which ye have delivered: and many such like things do ye.* Mark 7:13 There is absolutely no way the ruler of this world, Satan, would want anyone to have a relationship with the Almighty King and gain all the magnificent gifts and supernatural power He has available. It is a block to prevent connecting to God and is done deliberately and specifically through the lack of teaching of the Holy Spirit. Kingdom power is evident through the Holy Spirit.

When we have the Holy Spirit, we have God *living* within us who is the *key* to His Kingdom, literally. *In whom ye also trusted, after ye heard the word of truth, the gospel of your salvation: in whom also after that ye believed, <u>ye were sealed with the Holy Spirit</u> of promise.* Ephesians 1:13

Satan doesn't want you to gain supernatural power that can be used to deflect his wiles. He wants to keep you as far from God's truth as possible. Satan's focus is always to steal, kill, and destroy. He will steer you away from your Almighty King and destroy that which he can in your life easily under the disguise of lack of knowledge. Lack of Kingdom wisdom places you in unbelief. One of the numerous responsibilities of the Holy Spirit is to protect you from these attacks. You have a personal defender, but do you acknowledge Him? He is ready to defend and protect if you allow Him.

Key to the Kingdom

Let it sink into your soul this most precious wisdom that the Holy Spirit is your <u>key</u> to a relationship with your heavenly Father and entrance into His Almighty Kingdom. This is worth repeating! You are seated with Christ; therefore, ask on His authority and receive through the Holy Spirit. *And he that searcheth the hearts knoweth what is the mind of the Spirit, because he <u>maketh intercession for the saints</u> according to the will of God.* Romans 8:27

Upon receiving the Holy Spirit after your spirit birth in Christ, it is mandatory to quicken or awaken (baptism) the Holy Spirit. *But if the Spirit of him that raised up Jesus from the dead <u>dwell in you</u>, he that raised up Christ from the dead shall also <u>quicken your mortal bodies by his Spirit that dwelleth in you</u>.* Romans 8:11 As Christ has awakened your spirit, so do you need to awaken the Holy Spirit with a prayer of acknowledgement.

Here's an analogy that may help. If someone gives you a bank card as a gift, and you hold onto it without calling the number on the back to activate the card, but instead place it in your wallet, or throw it into a drawer, there are no benefits from the gift. The card is useless in making purchases.

Likewise, this is true of the Holy Spirit. You have the gift, but are you applying the benefits in your life? All it takes is praying to the Father that you accept His gift and ask that the Holy Spirit be an active participant in your life. It's that simple.

Father, thank you for sending your Son to free me from the bondage of sin, and as I am reborn in Christ, I am also thankful for the gift of the Holy Spirit. I come before you asking that the Holy Ghost be awakened within me, so that I may live and serve according to your Word. On the name of Christ and the blood He shed at Calvary for me, I pray, Amen.

Begin your spirit life with a heartfelt desire to love your Father and want a relationship with Him. Live according to His Kingdom principles and accept the presence of the Holy Spirit, so that all blessings are released when you pray, for God promises it.

As a newborn spirit person, the Holy Spirit removes the veil (parables) so that you read the Father's Word with spiritual eyes and learn of Him and His Kingdom. Your spiritual tutor will teach you all things of the spirit realm. *And he said unto them, <u>Unto you it is given to know the mystery of the kingdom of God</u>: but unto them that are without, all these things are done in parables: That seeing they may see, and not perceive; and hearing they may hear, and not understand; lest at any time they should be converted, and their sins should be forgiven them.* Mark 4:11-12

Words of God are solely for His children and this is why the Holy Spirit is also referred to as the Spirit of Truth. The Holy Spirit is your best friend, confidant, protector, provider, and advocate (spokesperson) before God. He is a valuable person in your life, for now you have His supernatural provisions. *Which things also we speak, not in the words which man's wisdom teacheth, but which the Holy Ghost teacheth; comparing spiritual things with spiritual.* 1 Corinthians 2:13

With a steadfast trust in the Holy Spirit, the communication *channel* is open to you. *Now the God of hope fill you with all joy and peace in believing, that ye may abound in hope, through the power of the Holy Ghost.* Romans 15:13 Believe in the friendship of the Holy Spirit and see Him as a person who is with you always looking out for your interest. Spend time conversing with Him as you would a dear friend.

Just as in friendship, you would not knowingly cause harm or grief, be cautious to not grieve the Holy Spirit. Don't allow soulful thoughts and behavior to interfere with your relationship. *And grieve not the Holy Spirit of God, whereby ye are sealed unto the day of redemption.* Ephesians 4:30

To know the things that fall into this category, the Holy Spirit tells us what He expects in our relationship with Him, so that we do not unbeknown grieve His presence. *That ye put off concerning the former conversation the old man, which is corrupt according to the deceitful lusts; And be renewed in the spirit of your mind; And that you put on the new man, which after God is created in righteousness and true holiness. Wherefore putting away lying, speaking every man truth with his neighbor: for we are members one of another. Be ye angry, and sin not: let not the sun go down upon your wrath: Neither give place to the devil. Let him that stole steal no more: but let him labour, working with his hands the thing which is good, that he may have to give to him that needeth. Let no corrupt communication proceed out of your mouth, but that which is good to the use of edifying, that it may minister grace unto the hearers. Let all bitterness, and wrath, and anger, and clamour, and evil speaking be put away from you, with all malice: And be ye kind one to another, tenderhearted, forgiving one another, even as God for Christ's sake hath forgiven you.* Ephesians 4:22-29; 31-32 The Holy Spirit makes it very clear how we are to conduct ourselves, which if you notice defines His *Fruits of the Spirit*, or principles for the spirit person.

Living in Peace

We are to be mindful of the *Fruit of the Spirit* as the Holy Spirit lives in our heart and not allow anger, bitterness, lack of forgiveness, hatred and so forth to influence our mind and behavior. As we wouldn't deliberately offend a friend, we surely should be mindful to not grieve God.

Choose to live a life for the Father within His Kingdom. Even born in Christ, if we fail to *crossover* from the carnal to a spirit life, we miss out on the precious gifts, healing, and supernatural power for they are meant for the spirit person.

It's so much more than having salvation; it is everything God has to give to you right now, today, but it requires learning how to live in two worlds simultaneously, natural and spirit, and allow your spirit to excel over your soul in all matters of life.

Summary of a Marriage Gift

But God, who is rich in mercy, for his great love wherewith he loved us, Even when we were dead in sins, hath quickened us together with Christ, (by grace ye are saved;) And hath raised us up together, and made us sit together in heavenly places in Christ Jesus: That in the ages to come he might shew the exceeding riches of his grace in his kindness toward us through Christ Jesus.
Ephesians 2:4-7

The Trinity of God is the Father, the Son, and the Holy Spirit, and He reveals each for a specific role in man's life. God is our Almighty King; however, He left His throne and came to the Kingdom of Earth born of flesh and became the Son to teach us about Himself. He came to claim the children born of the first Adam by becoming the second Adam.

Upon His return to the Kingdom, God gave all things both in Heaven and on earth to His beloved Son. In turn, Christ gives to you in joint-ownership the treasures within the Kingdom. These gifts are supplied to you through the third person of the Trinity that you may receive spiritual blessings for your earthen life.

When we accept Christ, we become married to Him for the Father. Therefore, as Christ is seated on the throne at the right hand of God, so are we with Him. *And hath raised us up together, and <u>made us sit together in heavenly places in Christ Jesus</u>: That in the ages to come he might shew the exceeding riches of his grace in his* *kindness toward us through Christ Jesus.* Ephesians 2:6-7 Nothing is withheld; however, we can obstruct the flow of the Kingdom power through our lack of knowledge, our grieving the Holy Spirit, and our misguided trust through unbelief.

God loves you so much He left His throne and came to a corrupt world to seek you out and bring you home. However, not against the free will He gave you, but allowing you to choose Him, to want Him to forever be your Father, your King.

TRINITY OF THE KINGDOM

And this is the confidence that we have in him, that, if we ask any thing according to his will, he heareth us: And if we know that he hear us, whatsoever we ask, we know that we have the petitions that we desired of him.
1 John 5:14-15

In any relationship there is mutual admiration, respect, and love from both individuals. This is defined as eros love in a marriage, storge love of parents for their children, and the affectionate love in friendship is philia. We know God's love is agape, an unconditional love. God's enduring love is expressed in His trinity of the Father, Son, and Holy Spirit; His love for man with the trinity of body, soul, and spirit; and His Almighty Kingdom functions with mercy, grace, and faith. It is noteworthy that three trinities have within them respectively three presentations.

In the beginning God created the heavens and the earth begins our study of the foundation of God's creation. In the generations captured in the Old Testament, we have the history of God's relationship with His chosen people, the Israelites. There is a foretelling of a shadow of things to come (Jesus), whereby throughout the Old Testament we see the representation of Christ. We witness the establishment of God's seven covenants and prophecies of His timeline and the events therein.

In the New Testament, we have God leaving His throne and coming to earth to provide a means that His children may return to Him for an eternal life, salvation is taught. What was spoken of in the Old Testament has become a reality in the New Testament in Christ.

Let's begin with the trinity of God. As just stated, God presents Himself to man as the Father, the Son, and the Holy Spirit. First within the Kingdom, it was God, the Word, and the Holy Ghost. God is all three, so why is it necessary to have three separate personages of Himself? Why not simply be God and leave it at that? Because each has a very specific purpose for man's life; each gives to man separately the requirements for a relationship with Him, from being born into the spirit realm (Christ), to living within the spirit Kingdom (Holy Spirit) as we continue to live in the natural world until we are resurrected to the Kingdom in our new bodies.

Our eternal spirit life begins the moment of our birth in Christ. Our commitment to live in the spirit defines our relationship with God. It starts with God and comes full circle from the Father through Christ and through the Holy Spirit back to God. We are connected to God through our spirit.

It is important to understand the purpose for each. For example, praying to be born into the spirit realm through the Holy Spirit will not give you a rebirth into the Kingdom. That is specifically the role of Christ. To pray to Christ for a healing or miracle does not render an answer because this is not provided in Christ, but through the Holy Spirit. Remember, Jesus performed no miracles or healing until the Holy Spirit came upon Him.

When Christ was on earth, He did everything as One because He was God and had the Holy Spirit. However, after ascending to the Kingdom of Heaven, everything comes to man through Christ's <u>authority</u> *and* the <u>provision</u> of the supernatural power of the Holy Spirit. Can you see why God established the trinity? Each is God, but each has a definitive role in man's life.

It is imperative to know the role of Christ and the Holy Spirit and their gifts, so that we may acquire spiritual things within the Kingdom. If we are unaware of the significance of God's presentation of Himself, our salvation is not affected: however, we miss the many blessings God has promised for our earthen life. There is a trinity to God, to man, and to the Kingdom.

Administering Kingdom Gifts

God and Christ's gifts are *administration* and *ministry* while the Holy Spirit's gifts are of *power*. It's necessary to acknowledge the gifts each presents, for there is a reason it is established this way. *Now concerning spiritual gifts brethren, I would not have you ignorant.* 1 Corinthians 12:1 And, *Now there are diversities of gifts, but the same Spirit. And there are differences of administrations, but the same Lord. And there are diversities of operations, but it is the same God which worketh all in all.* 1 Corinthians 12:4-6

God's gifts are administrative and all encompassing

in the function of His Kingdom. *Now ye are the body of Christ, and members in particular. And God hath set some in the church, first <u>apostles</u>, secondarily <u>prophets</u>, thirdly <u>teachers</u>, after that <u>miracles</u>, then gifts of <u>healings</u>, <u>helps</u>, <u>governments</u>, <u>diversities of tongues</u>. are all apostles? are all prophets? are all teachers? are all workers of miracles? Have all the gifts of healing? do all speak with tongues? do all interpret? But covet earnestly the best gifts: and yet show I unto you a more excellent way.* 1 Corinthians 12:27-31 We can see the inclusion of the gifts of Christ and the Holy Spirit within God's gifts. God appoints His gifts to man through the Holy Spirit.

When God came to earth to be born in human form as the second person of the Trinity, the Son, He had a specific purpose to fulfill. He was already acknowledged as a King from another world. *For unto you is born this day in the city of David a Saviour, which is Christ the Lord. And this shall be a sign unto you; Ye shall find the babe wrapped in swaddling clothes, lying in a manger. And suddenly there was with the angel a multitude of the heavenly host praising God, and saying, Glory to God in the highest, and on earth peace, good will toward men.* Luke 2:11-14

When Jesus was a young boy of twelve, He unofficially began His ministry; however, it is dutifully noted in the Scriptures that He officially started teaching once baptized with the Holy Spirit at the age of thirty. *And when he was twelve years old, they went up to Jerusalem after the custom of the feast. And when they had fulfilled the days, as they returned, the child Jesus tarried behind in Jerusalem; and Joseph and his mother knew not it.* Luke 2:42-43 Also, *And it came to pass, that after three days they found him in the temple, sitting in the midst of the doctors, both hearing them, and asking them questions. And all that heard them were astonished at his understanding and answers.* Luke 2:46-47

When His parents found Him in the temple, they were surprised where He was and amazed at the knowledge He spoke. Can you imagine this scene; here's a young boy who typically would not have permission to be in the temple or synagogue, nor to have the privilege of a conversation with prominent people, and yet, there He sat amongst them conversing with a greater intellect than their own. When they questioned their son, Jesus replied to them: *And he said unto them, How is it that ye sought me? Wist ye not that I must be about my Father's business? And they understood not the saying which he spoke unto them.* Luke 2:49-50

Upon their return to Nazareth, Jesus' wisdom grew. *And Jesus increased in wisdom and stature, and in favour with God and man.* Luke 2:52 We don't have an account of how Jesus spent His years from age twelve to thirty before His baptism with the Holy Spirit. We do know His knowledge, wisdom, and favor with God and man increased.

It is logical to assume that Jesus did not withhold knowledge but often communicated with the prominent people of His day just as He did in the temple in Jerusalem. It would appear that His ministry truly began at the age of twelve in Jerusalem, and the place Christ will return as our King.

When Christ was baptized by John the Baptist in Jordan, He received the Holy Spirit and openly taught of the Kingdom of Heaven and God the Father, while performing miracles and healing. *And it came to pass in those days, that Jesus came from Nazareth of Galilee, and was baptized of John in Jordan. And straightway coming up out of the water, he saw the heavens opened, and the Spirit like a dove descending upon him: And there came a voice from heaven, saying, Thou art my beloved Son, in whom I am well pleased.* Mark 1:9-11

Jesus was the age of thirty when He began speaking to the multitude gathered to hear Him. *And Jesus himself began to be about thirty years of age (as was supposed) the son of Joseph, which was the son of Hedi.* Luke 3:23 His first miracle was at the wedding in Cana when He changed water to wine. *This beginning of miracles did Jesus in Cana in Galilee, and manifested forth his glory, and his disciples believed on him.* John 2:11

Jesus' ministry lasted three years once He received the power of the Holy Spirit. It is noteworthy that even Jesus did not perform miracles or teach of the Kingdom of Heaven until after He received the Holy Spirit. This holds true today of the importance of the Holy Spirit in our lives. As supernatural heavenly power came to the man Jesus from the Father, so today the same Holy Spirit comes to you. We can see the relevancy for Him in our life, for He is God.

God came to be the Good Shepard gathering the flock (lost children through sin) and enable them to have a means of returning to their heavenly Father. He performed miracles and healing to prove His truth. To remove the sins from the physical man, He would need to be of flesh; and thus, bore the sins and transgressions of man upon His own body on the Cross at Calvary. *For Christ also hath once suffered for sins, the just for the unjust, that he might bring us to God, being put to death in the flesh, but quickened by the Spirit.* 1 Peter 3:18 All iniquities and infirmities were destroyed, *put to death*, on the Cross in Christ.

Authority in Christ

When Christ returned to the Kingdom, He provided numerous benefits for man: our spirit birth through His Spirit; He gives us the gift of the Holy Spirit; He gives us a marriage to Himself allowing us to be joint-heirs or co-owners within the Kingdom and as such we are seated with Christ whereby we may call upon His authority for all heavenly treasures and power. Christ is always with us and we are with Him! Nothing is lacking, not even an unanswered prayer.

As Christ sits at the right hand of the Father, all things within the Kingdom are through the *authority* in Him, which is not the same as saying that everything is *provided* by Christ. It is imperative to differentiate between the purpose of Christ and the purpose of the Holy Spirit. The authority is in Christ; however, the provision is in the Holy Spirit. This is important; *authority* and *provision*. If you are praying and expecting Christ to answer, this is not His role in your life. Though your prayer must be on the authority of Christ, it is rendered through the Holy Spirit, the supernatural power within the Kingdom. For example, concluding your prayer with: *Thank you, Father. On your Son, Jesus' name I pray and through the provision of the Holy Spirit, Amen.*

Christ's gifts are ministerial. *Now that he ascended, what is it but that he also descended first into the lower parts of the earth? He that descended is the same also* *that ascended up far above all heavens, that he might fill all things. And he gave some, <u>apostles</u>; and some, <u>prophets</u>; and some, <u>evangelists</u>; and some, <u>pastors</u> and <u>teachers</u>; For the perfecting of the saints, for the work of the ministry, for the edifying of the body of Christ.* Ephesians 4:9-12 If our dependance on Christ is for answered prayers, we can see that His gifts are not provisional. They are for the continuation of His ministry.

Though we have many doctrines, pastors, preachers, priests, and theologians today, it does not mean they are all called by Christ to continue His ministry. There are many professing the Word of God who have not been anointed by Christ.

However, once we have the truth of God's Word as discerned through the Holy Spirit, we will be able to recognize false teachings. Just as Christ's disciples went forth anointed with the Holy Spirit to teach the gospel as taught to them by Jesus, we also hold a position as joint-heirs in Christ to be <u>stewards</u> of His Word, <u>disciples</u> in the administration, and <u>ambassadors</u> to the truth.

When we address the third person of the Trinity of God, the Holy Spirit, we learn He has many roles with the most obvious to unite us to our heavenly Father. Our spirit birth is in Christ; however, our relationship is established through the Holy Spirit, for from the beginning He is our tutor of God's Word.

As you are a parent who give gifts to your children, so does our heavenly Father have gifts for you. *If ye then, being evil know how to give good gifts unto your children: how much more shall your heavenly Father give the Holy Spirit to them that ask him?* Luke 11:13 The Holy Spirit gives the most gifts because all Kingdom promises and power are fulfilled through the third person of the

Trinity of God.

Wisdom in the Holy Spirit

In the Holy Spirit, God has provided all that we will need for our spirit life. *But the manifestation of the Spirit is given to every man to profit withal. For to one is given by the Spirit the word of <u>wisdom</u>; to another the word of <u>knowledge</u> by the same Spirit; To another <u>faith</u> by the same Spirit; to another the gifts of <u>healing</u> by the same Spirit; To another the working of <u>miracles</u>; to another <u>prophecy</u>; to another <u>discerning of spirits</u>; to another <u>divers kinds of tongues</u>; to another the <u>interpretation of tongues</u>: But all these work that one and the selfsame Spirit, dividing to every man severally as he will.* 1 Corinthians 12:7-11

Notice faith, healing, miracles, wisdom, and knowledge are all given through the Holy Spirit. There is nothing lacking in what we may receive through His provisions. *Again, the kingdom of heaven is like unto treasure hid in a field; the which when a man hath found, he hideth, and for joy thereof goeth and selleth all that he hath, and buyeth that field.* Matthew 13:44

Can you begin to see the magnificent beauty of how God set everything within His Kingdom for you? It is the most awesome love story ever told, for it is all about you, the subject of His desires. God wants to fellowship with you. In your trust and reliance on the Holy Spirit, you can expect an answer to your prayer, for God promises it, and for every promise there is a provision.

Once we understand the trinity of God for the trinity

of man, there are requirements of the Holy Spirit that we abide in. These are referred to as the Fruits of the Spirit. *But the fruit of the Spirit is love, joy, peace, longsuffering, gentleness, goodness, faith, meekness, temperance: against such there is no law.* Galatians 5:22-23 When we renew our thinking, we replace the carnal negative emotions of anger, hate, disillusionment, disappointment, fear, worry, and so on with the *Fruit of the Holy Spirit.* In our heart we have peace, joy, love, faith, goodness, kindness, and so forth. With these, we conduct our behavior. Think of it as new management who has brought their guidelines into the operation of a business. In this case, you are the new creation in Christ, and the Holy Spirit is the new management with His expectations of your conduct.

Though we have been born in Christ for a relationship with the Father, it requires our continuous fellowship through the Holy Spirit for a true commitment to God. If we are not living a spirit to Spirit life daily, then the very lack in our relationship with God is a position of taking Him for granted; to only call upon Him in time of need. God is not a part-time provider; meaning, we only have need of Him in a crisis but aren't nurturing a relationship. This behavior on our part is another example how we block the flow of His provisions.

Those who fall within this category probably don't realize they are doing so, but if they're believing minimally of His provisions and doubt His abilities to give, then the relationship is not intimate with the Father. The benefits occur with our commitment. <u>*If ye abide in me, and my words abide in you, ye shall ask what ye will, and it shall be done unto you*</u>. John 15:7

Our relationship is only as trustworthy as our faith in

the Holy Spirit. We can have an awareness of God and Christ, but not be knowledgeable of the Kingdom precepts. We are responsible for the lack of God's greatness in our life. As a joint-heir in Christ, we have co-ownership within the Kingdom, something to be mindful of.

Mercy, Grace, and Faith

With the trinity of God and the trinity of man, there is also the trinity of the Kingdom. This is referring to the functionality of the Kingdom of Heaven which is mercy, grace, and faith. Knowing the nature of God and His love, we should give attention to the principles that govern His Kingdom.

For example, each country has a parliament or governmental structure as does the Kingdom of Heaven. Beginning with mercy, we may consider it the platform, or base that grace and faith is expressed. *But God, who is <u>rich in mercy</u>, for his great love wherewith he loved* us. Ephesians 2:4 Consider the soil when you bury a seed and the seed grows into a plant. Perhaps, mercy can be likened to the soil, for God's mercy is present no matter the disobedience of His children. Mercy has always been at the forefront of God's Kingdom.

Webster's dictionary defines mercy as the compassionate or kindly forbearance shown towards an offender, an enemy, or other person under one's influences; an act of kindness or favor, something that gives evidence of divine favor; blessing. This is precisely what God gives to man.

In His love, we experience His mercy. Just like the mercy that is given to a prodigal child who has strayed, the love always remains. It was mercy God gave to the Israelites in their disobedience when He removed them from bondage in Egypt. *Thou in thy mercy hast led forth the people which thou hast redeemed: thou hast guided them in thy strength unto thy holy habitation.* Exodus 15:13

Without God's mercy, how would we experience grace and faith? *And he said, I will make all my goodness pass before thee, and I will proclaim the name of the Lord before thee; and will be gracious to whom I will be gracious, and will show mercy on whom I will show mercy.* Exodus 33:19 God's mercy never changes and is for the saved and unsaved because it is established within His Kingdom as the foundation for grace and faith. *Not by works of righteousness we have done, but according to his mercy he saved us, by the washing of regeneration, and renewing of the Holy Ghost.* Timothy 3:5 Without God's mercy, man would not exist. It is His compassion for mankind.

An analogy to living in the mercy of God is likened to an insurance policy; however, there is no better life insurance, health coverage, or retirement benefits than with God. His provisions never expire, and we are guaranteed physical and emotional healing, provided prosperity, and given eternal life. We are far greater than the angels, for we are God's children. *Keep yourselves in the love of God, looking for the mercy of our Lord Jesus Christ unto eternal life.* Jude 1:21

God's mercy is the love and patience He expresses continuously to man. His mercy is constant without degree or dimension. It is always in place, a perfect expression of love. *For the Lord is good; his mercy is everlasting; and his truth endureth to all generations.* Psalm 100:5 To have mercy or compassion towards someone who has done an injustice is a remarkable act of kindness. God shows mercy towards a sinful people.

Once we understand the mercy of God upon all His people, then grace is evident. Grace is a gift of pardon and forgiveness. Grace existed in the generations within the Old Testament era, for grace is of the Kingdom, and as God extended His mercy, He also gave grace (forgiveness). Some examples are Noah and Moses. *But Noah found <u>grace in the eyes of the Lord</u>.* Genesis 6:8 Also, *And the Lord said unto Moses, I will do this thing also that thou hast spoken: <u>for thou hast found grace in my sight</u>, and I know thee by name.* Exodus 33:17

God showed grace to those who were faithful to Him. With the new covenant in Christ, grace is freely given to all who believe in Him, taking on the righteousness of Christ. *For the law was given to Moses, but <u>grace and truth came by Jesus Christ</u>.* John 1:17 Also, *Grace be with you, mercy, and peace, from God the Father, and from the Lord Jesus Christ, the Son of the Father, in truth and love.* 2 John 1:3 Grace is always present; however, our carnal thoughts and lack of commitment can easily cause us to slip out of God's provision of grace. We still have forgiveness but the blessings can be restricted.

It is because of His grace that we may acquire God's many gifts. *But unto <u>every one of us is given grace</u> according to the measure of the gift of Christ.* Ephesians 4:7 Christ removed our sins, whereby we live in grace. *Being justified freely by his grace through the redemption that is in Christ Jesus.* Romans 3:24 This is not a free ticket to sin but should we slip and commit an act that grieves God, we acknowledge our misconduct. Forgiveness is present in grace, not in the law.

Just as you would forgive your child for a disobedience to you, so does our heavenly Father forgive our trespasses. *For sin shall not have dominion over you: for ye are not under the law, but under grace.* Romans 6:14 Take note of the terminology: *but under grace.* Upon our birth into the Kingdom, we live in grace. Grace is always present whereby we are conscious of the gift of grace. *I thank my God always on your behalf, for the grace of God is given you by Jesus Christ.* 1 Corinthians 1:4

With our Father's mercy and grace, we live in faith to His Word. Faith is also a gift of the Holy Spirit; therefore, God gives mercy, grace, and faith. Notice that God supplies everything man requires including faith. He has made it very easy for man, for what is required on our part is having the faith equivalent to a mustard seed, such a minimal amount. God has done everything; therefore, with belief we hold our trust in faith.

Notice how faith begets grace. As we live spiritually within the Kingdom, we know it is the gift of faith that enables us to have a relationship with God and to receive His blessings in our life though His grace. When we show our faith, it enables the Holy Spirit to witness our faith by His faith within the Kingdom.

God's mercy, grace, and faith is constant upon His children. *Without faith it is impossible to please God.* Hebrews 11:6 It should become our desire to obtain wisdom in our Father's Word enabling us to walk uprightly in Christ by faith. *For by grace are ye saved through faith; and that not of yourselves: it is the gift of God: Not of works, lest any man should boast.* Ephesians

2:8-9 God's loving and forgiving nature as shown in His mercy (compassion) with grace (forgiveness) is fulfilled in faith. *By whom also <u>we have access by faith into this grace wherein we stand</u>, and rejoice in hope of the glory of God.* Romans 5:2 It is noteworthy to understand the semantics of how our faith releases grace.

Though mercy and grace are foundational within the Kingdom, and the faith of the Holy Spirit is a gift, it is our faith that secures grace. An analogy would be likened to a cell phone. If we have not taken the time to read the manual that came with the new device, but instead operate the phone based on our perception of how it works, we can miss many of its features. Just because we haven't made ourselves privy to the various pre-programmed applications, doesn't mean they aren't accessible on the phone.

Same holds true with faith. We receive the gift and are expected to study the manual, the Bible, to learn how faith operates in the Kingdom, so we will not be without the blessings that come through faith. We are to know how to allocate faith to release grace like a combination to a lock. *Let us therefore come boldly unto the <u>throne of grace</u> that we may obtain mercy, and find grace to help in time of need.* Hebrews 4:16

God's grace is omnipresent, but we can obstruct its function. Faith is more than believing God is our heavenly Father, for it is how we access the Kingdom. Through faith, our trust is expressed within our spirit person to the Spirit of God through the Spirit of Truth.

When we ask to be born into God's Kingdom, He expects us to accept a covenant in His Son and receive the gift of the Holy Spirit. Our objective is to live by His Kingdom principles and allow the *Fruit of the Spirit* to abide in our heart and be the guidepost for our daily behavior. Our desire is an intimate relationship with our Father and trust Him implicitly.

As we mature in knowledge and wisdom of God's Kingdom, we give thanksgiving and glory always to our Father for the blessings He bestows upon our life as we live as a *spirit* person to His *Spirit* within the *spirit* Kingdom of Heaven.

Summary of the Trinity of the Kingdom

And I will give unto thee the keys of the kingdom of heaven: and whatsoever thou shalt bind on earth shall be bound in heaven: and whatsoever thou shalt loose on earth shall be loosed in heaven.
Matthew 16:19

In wisdom of our Almighty King and His Kingdom, we mature in His Word as the Holy Spirit unveils His plan, purpose, and role for man's life. We also know our King as the Father, the Son, and the Holy Spirit who has given man a body, soul, and spirit while His Kingdom functions with mercy, grace and faith. Our spirit person requires the Spirit of Truth concerning all matters within the Kingdom.

We witness the magnitude of how history unfolds in both the Old Testament under the law and in the New Testament in grace. In the Old era, God spoke with the people directly, while Christ is evident in the New

Testament as He was among the people. God's wrath was understood under the law for the sins of man; however, grace is given in Christ whereby sin has been removed.

As a spirit person born into the Kingdom of Heaven, accept grace and not be held in bondage under the old covenant law of Moses through man's traditions. Grace will supply Kingdom blessings, while the law holds you captive to a sin nature. God set forth His Kingdom as an eternal home and there is no sin present.

It truly depends on each of us to garner the wisdom to receive from the Kingdom of Heaven. God is never withholding His promises, nor is He dispensing wrath. Born of His Son, we live in the inherited righteousness of Christ.

When we ask through our intercessor, the Holy Spirit, professing our faith and believing the answer is forthcoming, our one fervent prayer spoken with thanksgiving in belief enables the supernatural power. Instead of continual pleading and wondering if God will answer, pray that you have received. This is the difference in prayers being answered because you show trust in Him. Wondering is unbelief. Praising the Father with thanksgiving is saying: *thank you for helping me*. That's all He wants to hear. Within these few words, He sees your faith. That's all God desires.

Praise, glory, honor, and thanksgiving to our Most High God, our Almighty King, our heavenly Father.

Amen and Amen!

COMMUNION IN CHRIST

Therefore we are buried with him by baptism into death: that like as Christ was raised up from the dead by the glory of the Father, even so we also should walk in newness of life.
Romans 6:4

When Christ returned to the Kingdom of Heaven, he didn't leave us empty-handed. He taught twelve men to continue in His place, but it doesn't end there. If it did and once these men died, who would carry on henceforth? His teaching would eventually die with them, and no one would know of God and His Kingdom.

God's divine plan included a means that all men would have equal opportunity to know Him. God selected individuals who were called prophets and told them what to write. *<u>As it is written in the prophets</u>, Behold, I send my messenger before thy face, which shall prepare thy way before thee.* Mark 1:2 These writings are referred to as Scriptures and are first noted in the Torah (Hebrew), translated to Greek, and finally to our English Bible.

Christ referred to what had been written in His many references when questioned by the Pharisees, priests, and even His disciples. *But he answered and said, <u>It is</u>*

written, *Man shall not live by bread alone, but by every word that proceedeth out of the mouth of God.* Matthew 4:4 Remember, Christ is the *Word* who manifested all God's work. Thus, He is speaking to the people of Himself. Many times He would refer to: *It is written,* exemplifying what will always remain without change.

Another example is when Satan tempted Jesus right after He received the Holy Spirit and was in the wilderness for forty days. *Then saith Jesus unto him, Get thee hence, Satan: for* _it is written_, *Thou shalt worship the Lord thy God, and him only shalt thou serve.* Matthew 4:10 Christ is the Word, and the written word was of Him that the prophets spoke of; and thus, Jesus stated often, *It is written,* because He spoke of what God and Himself established in the beginning.

Christ is the Son of Man, but He is also the Son of God in His holy deity. Therefore, nothing is without His knowledge and this is why He always replied: *It is written,* just as His last words were, *It is finished*.

So when His work in this earthen Kingdom was finished and He returned to His throne, what did He leave for man? Our Messiah left Himself to anyone who believes in who He is and from where He came.

How was He able to leave of Himself when we know He ascended back to the Kingdom? And, since this was nearly two-thousand years ago when He made an appearance on earth, what do we have of Him today? We would naturally answer these questions by saying we have the Scriptures that teach of who He is. This is true; however, traditional studies have a tendency to focus on the name of Jesus rather than the personages of Son of God and of Man. To know Christ, it is necessary to see the two personages presented to man on man's behalf.

He became the beloved Son of God and the sacrificial Son of Man. The Son of Man, His human person who died on the Cross, represents the life of man, the carnal man. It is the Son of Man who was tortured, crucified, and killed for teaching a truth the priests didn't understand or want. The Son of Man was the sacrificial Lamb of God.

As more and more people were listening and following His teachings, it frightened the priests who went to their king complaining. They were fearful the people would no longer adhere to their beliefs and they would lose their power over them. In their humanistic thought, something had to be done with Jesus.

However, the Son of God with Kingdom wisdom knew what was to be, for it was in the plan. He spoke to His disciples of coming from another world to earth to finish His Father's work. *Jesus saith unto them, My meat is to do the will of him that sent me, and to finish his work.* John 4:34 Also, *But Jesus answered them, My Father worketh hitherto, and I work.* John 5:17

When Jesus was a boy of twelve years and was found by his parents in a synagogue, after not finding Him for three days in the camp traveling home, they questioned Him. His reply was: *And he said unto them, How is it that ye sought me? wist ye not that I must be about my Father's business?* Luke 2:49 Even as a boy, Yeshua knew His place and purpose for being on earth.

Before His execution, He took His disciples to a mountaintop and spoke to them of things that would soon occur, but they didn't understand. He told them He would be leaving them, but they wouldn't be left alone. Afterwards, the night before they came for Him when He ate the last meal (Lord's Supper) with His twelve men in the Upper Room in Jerusalem, He explained what He was leaving with them. *And as they were eating, Jesus took bread, and blessed it, and brake it, and gave it to the disciples, and said, take, eat; this is my body. And he took the cup, and gave thanks, and gave it to them, saying, Drink ye all of it; For this is my blood of the new testament, which is shed for many for the remission of sins.* Matthew 26:26-28 Jesus gave His disciples a final instruction and a most compelling one. However, they didn't grasp the symbolism of the bread and wine.

Also in the Book of Luke: *And he took bread, and gave thanks, and brake it, and gave unto them, saying, This is my body which is given for you: this do in remembrance of me. Likewise also the cup after supper, saying, This cup is the new testament in my blood, which is shed for you.* Luke 22:19-20 It was difficult for them to comprehend all the things Jesus wanted them to know before He left His men on their own.

Jesus was explaining the representation of His body and His blood as a sacrifice (Lamb of God), for a new covenant for all mankind upon His death on the Cross. He was giving Himself that we may always be in remembrance of Him and what He has done for man.

Throughout the many generations to follow, it is something to give great homage to once united with Him in Spirit. Born of His Spirit, you are intimately connected with the Son of the Most High God. Christ is our Lord.

Before Jesus surrendered Himself for the imminent crucifixion, He told them to return to the Upper Room and wait for the Comforter whom He would send. This is where Christ was with them before His death, and where

He returned and spent time with them upon His resurrection before ascending to the throne.

Ten days later, for a total of fifty days from Christ's resurrection, they were all endued with supernatural Kingdom power of the Holy Spirit. The Son of God equipped His men with the same power He possessed while the Son of Man. They were now prepared to continue His ministry of the Kingdom.

Upon the Son of Man's last breath on the Cross, the veil which separated God and man was ripped in two removing the wall (sin) that kept man from God. The Son of Man died as a human person in our place on the Cross and bore our iniquities that we may become a child in the Kingdom of Heaven. Our only way to our Most High God, our Almighty King, our Father is through the means that God provided and that is the *Word* becoming the Son of God, the Son of Man, the second person of the Trinity of God.

When the Son of God returned to the throne, what did He give to man? Notice the difference in the persons of the Son of God and Son of Man. Son of Man *did* for man, while Son of God *gives* to man. We shouldn't jumble everything into one concept of Christ's work. Though we know of so much He did while on earth, there is even greater that He gives to each person who trust Him. So what does the Son of God give to the newborn child of the Father?

The Son of God gives His Spirit, His righteousness, His holiness, His authority, and supernatural Kingdom power through the Holy Spirit. He gives grace and truth. His grace is forever flowing into our life. *And of His fullness we have all received, and grace for grace. For the law was given through Moses, but grace and truth came through Jesus Christ.* John 1:16-17 It is His grace that supplies for all our needs.

We were born self-righteous; however, in our rebirth in Christ's Spirit, we inherit His righteousness. We are as He is, righteous. *Herein is our love made perfect, that we may have boldness in the day of judgment: because <u>as he is, so are we in this world</u>.* 1 John 4:17

As Christ is seated at the right hand of the Father to whom the Father has given all things both in Heaven and on Earth; we are as He is right now. Christ gives you His authority to ask of Him and He will answer, supplied through the Holy Spirit. *If ye shall ask any thing in my name, I will do it.* Romans 14:14 Could there be anything more gracious than this? Yes, even with all that the Son of God has done and given to man, there is also the gift of heavenly supernatural power. Amazing! He gives you even more…His power!

Absolutely nothing has been withheld from the child of God, because it was all meant for you from the very beginning. It has and will remain… *all about you.* The summation is this: the Son of God gave of Himself not only as a sacrifice on the Cross, but now in the Kingdom continues to give of Himself in position, authority, and power to all who believe in Him through trust and faith.

The next obvious thought is how do we release all that the Son of God has given? The answer may surprise you. Mindful of the difference between a carnal and spirit life, and maintaining wisdom in God's Word with trust and faith, it is simply a matter of praise. The answer is to praise the Son before the Father. Acknowledge all that the Son of God <u>did</u> and <u>gives</u> to make it possible for you, a sinner destined for death, to be redeemed. Praising the Son to the Father pleases God. As He calls

Christ His beloved Son, so then does He claim you as His beloved child, for in His Son, the Father sees you.

As a child of the Father, if you could grasp and hold to this knowledge, your life would be so different than what you may be enduring in your daily circumstances. Christ's authority releases the power of the Holy Spirit into your life. How else do you expect to receive a healing, or miracle if you haven't first acknowledged the principle that as Christ is in the Kingdom of Heaven, and He is in you in Spirit, so are you with Him in the Kingdom in spirit.

Born in Him, you are now where He is, and He is with you wherever you may be. Birthed with His Spirit and on His holy Name, you have His authority to ask of Him and receive. His last words as the Son of Man were: *It is finished.* Therefore, *I have glorified thee on the earth: I have finished the work which thou gavest me to do. John 17:4* Everything the Son of God and the Son of Man has accomplished is so you can be a child of the Most High God.

THE POWER OF PRAYER

And all things, whatsoever ye shall ask in prayer, believing, ye shall receive.
Matthew 21:22

We should consider our prayer before we speak. We pray in churches, weddings, funerals, social events, and even at mealtime each in a group or congregational gathering. Some believe prayer is more powerful when performed among others. *And when thou prayest, thou shalt not be as the hypocrites are: for they love to pray standing in the synagogues and in the corners of the streets, that they may be seen of men.* Matthew 6:5 It can be comforting and beneficial to participate in joint-worship; however, God requires we come to Him personally.

Prayer is a very intimate time with God, and He has given the Holy Spirit for our communion. The Holy Spirit is our intercessor before the Lord and presents our prayer. God hears our prayers, but the response we receive from the Kingdom is dependent upon the Holy Spirit. The Holy Spirit will render our prayer spiritually acceptable according to Kingdom laws, and the answer forthcoming is based on our unwavering faith and trust.

There is never a circumstance that God does not know about and has a provision in place. *Be not ye therefore like unto them; for your Father knoweth what things ye have need of, before ye ask him.* Matthew 6:8 Do we truly understand the value of a prayer, and how important it is that our petitions are accurate to God's Word, so that we may receive an expected answer?

We refresh our knowledge of what God declares: *But when ye pray, use not vain repetitions, as the heathen do: for they think that they shall be heard for their much speaking.* Matthew 6:7 It is a common mistake to take certain biblical scriptures, memorize them and repeat often. This according to God is not praying, and He says beware of doing such. We have His example in the Lord's Prayer. It seems when we want to pray to our Father, we turn to this prayer and recite it verbatim. In doing so, we believe we have covered all the bases and prayed as God intended. The Lord's Prayer is given to teach what we are to take into account.

Simply reciting this prayer when convenient does not constitute praying. Let's break it down, so we may understand what God is teaching. *Our Father which are in heaven, Hallowed be thy name, Thy kingdom come, Thy will be done in earth, as it is in heaven. Give us our daily bread. And forgive us our debts, as we forgive our debtors. And lead us not into temptation, but deliver us from evil: For thine is the kingdom, and the power, and the glory, for ever. Amen.* Matthew 6:9-13 God is telling us how to pray.

We begin our prayer acknowledging our Father with glory, honor, praise, and thanksgiving. What God has established within His Kingdom for man can and should be accomplished on earth as He has met our every need. Give us our daily bread is His provision for our life that our faith and trust rest in Him. For God says we are not to be concerned for what we eat, wear, or where we live for He provides for His children. We ask forgiveness of our sins and as we know ourselves to be forgiven in Christ, we are to forgive others that do us harm.

God tells us to turn our cheek the other way in forgiveness, and if harm persists, we are to walk away. *But I say unto you, That ye resist not evil: but whosoever shall smite thee on thy right cheek, turn to him the other also.* Matthew 5:39 Also, those that take from you, rather than fight for your possessions, give to them freely. *And unto him that smitten thee on the one cheek offer also the other; and him that taketh away thy cloak forbid not to take thy coat also.* Luke 6:29 We seek His guidance and ask for protection from the evil of this fallen world. Most importantly, we are to affirm that our faith is always in Him, His heavenly Kingdom, for it is forever.

Remember, whatever we may bring to God has already been provided for, so it is by faith we pray, for our benefit, not His. It is with obedience to His Word that our prayer releases in the Kingdom the resolution we seek. The blessings will manifest into the natural, or physical realm when we hold with conviction in belief with the faith of a mustard seed. Therefore, pray to the Father with thanksgiving, seek Him always, and rely only on Him for an effectual, fervent prayer avails much.

PRAYER TO THE FATHER

Even unto them will I give in mine house and within my walls a place and a name better than of sons and of daughters: I will give them an everlasting name, that shall not be cut off.
Isaiah 56:5

Father,

I come to you knowing my life is not as you meant for it to be, and I bear the responsibility of allowing worldly influences to dictate and dilute my thoughts, separating me from your presence and plan. I repent of my sins and transgressions and ask forgiveness for being unfaithful to you. Through my weakness, pride, and self-righteousness, I did not accept your Word, nor seek you for understanding and completion of who I am.

I present myself before you to be reborn into the spirit person you created me to be. I choose life with your Son and accept the gift of the Holy Ghost. You gave your Son, Jesus, that I may have salvation, but I also receive His death at Calvary for my wellbeing, healed by His stripes.

I believe:

- You love me so much, you left your Kingdom and came to earth in Christ to claim me as your own; giving your Son to die for me.

- You have a plan for my life before I was in the womb, not yet born.

- Jesus has given me a rebirth in spirit fusing His Spirit to mine, and I am reunited to you, my Father. With the authority of Christ and the gift of the Holy Spirit, I am adopted as your child, made a saint and heir in the Kingdom of Heaven.

- The Holy Spirit will teach me all things of the Kingdom, so that I receive knowledge, understanding, wisdom, and discernment of your Word. He will be my intercessor, tutor, and advocate before you.

- Through the Holy Spirit, I come before your throne in prayer and receive your heavenly gifts and power as I live in honor and glory to you, my heavenly Father and Almighty King.

- As my Father, I know you will be there for me. I am forgiven and never forsaken, and your mercy and grace are always present.

- In faith, I will be obedient and hold the truth in your Word.

- I have everlasting life with you and your Son.

- I am your child who one day will be given a new body to live forever in your Kingdom.

I know my prayers will be answered because your Word is a Living Word and responds to the Holy Spirit for the glory of your Kingdom. Thank you, Father, for loving me, forgiving me, and providing for my life. I praise, glorify, and give thanksgiving to you always. On the blood of your Son, Jesus, and through the Holy Spirit, I pray, Amen.

PORTRAIT OF MAN

So God created man in his own image, in the image of God created he him; male and female created he them.
Genesis 1:27

Our linage in the Kingdom of Heaven begins with God's creation of Adam, made of the earth, and man born of the seed of Adam onto the earth. The second Adam, Christ, redeems man from his sinful nature and gives us a new birth in spirit which returns us to the Kingdom. In God's portrait of the cycle of man's life, we come full circle.

    Man is made in God's image
    Man is made for God's pleasure
    Man is made to be God's children
    Man is made to be God's temple on Earth
    Man is made with a plan for his life
    God gives man the gift of Christ
    God gives man the gift of the Holy Spirit
    God gives man the gifts of mercy, grace, faith
    God gives man a free will to choose Him
    God gives man salvation, eternal life

SUMMARY

When we think of the Kingdom of Heaven, do we truly understand what is to be considered? It is a spiritual kingdom whereby we have the hope that our faith is strong to hold in the truth of God's Word. There is much to put our imagination to envision such as the throne of God, the mansions for the saints, the angels, and so forth.

Though there is no time in God's Kingdom, what do you suppose occurs in the reference of a day? What must it be like for the Father and the Son seated on the throne looking down on earth and watching His people? And to imagine that God knew us before we were conceived in our mother's womb, knows every hair on our head, and has a plan for our life. It's enough to boggle the mind, for our brain isn't capable of such an imagination of this magnificence or magnitude; and yet, we have been wonderfully made by God for the Father's pleasure.

God wanted to fill His Kingdom with children and we are those children born of His Son, cleansed of our corruptible sinful nature, robed in His righteousness, and made presentable for a pure and holy place. What is so truly magnificent is that it isn't a future tense but begins the very day we accept Christ's death on the Cross. It all begins at the Cross and carries through to eternity. It isn't a matter of believing and wait. When we believe in the Son of God, we begin a new spiritual life as a spirit-born person in Christ and learn to live in a spirit realm, the Kingdom of Heaven.

This is why God gives Himself to be our tutor to teach us how to live in His world, His Kingdom. We may still be *in* this earthen world; however, we are no longer *of* the world. All our provisions are supplied, our needs will be taken care of, for we will lack for nothing; however, they are spiritual gifts and blessings. We learn how to live in grace whereby all heavenly supernatural power is available to the children of the Father.

Our position as a child of God is simple. Like any child to a parent, the child depends on the parent to protect and provide for them, to love them, unconditionally. Because our heavenly Father is always expressing His love for us, we turn to Him in trust and faith. Therefore, we should desire to be in fellowship with Him daily, talking to Him about our concerns and when we pray, it is such an automatic occurrence with much thanksgiving and glory to the Father.

We don't need to plead with Him over any matter, for He knows our needs. God simply wants us to trust Him as our Father. We best do this by speaking our problem or concern and then letting Him resolve the matter.

There isn't anything more pleasing to God than His children desiring to communicate with Him with a trusting heart of love. We love because He first loved us, so we should honor His love with faithfulness.

SCRIPTURES

Matthew 13:44 Again, the kingdom of heaven is like unto treasure hid in a field; the which when a man hath found, he hideth, and for joy thereof goeth and selleth all that he hath, and buyeth that field.

Romans 8:26 Likewise the spirit also helpeth our infirmities: for we know not what we should pray for as we ought: but the spirit itself maketh intercession for us with groanings which cannot be uttered.

1 Corinthians 6:20 For ye are bought with a price: therefore glorify God in your body, and in your spirit, which are God's.

1 Corinthians 2:12 Now we have received, not the spirit of the world, but the spirit which is of God; that we might know the things that are freely given to us of God.

1 Corinthians 3:18-19 Let no man deceive himself. If any man among you seemeth to be wise in this world, let him become a fool, that he may be wise. For the wisdom of this world is foolishness with God. For it is written, He taketh the wise in their own craftiness.

John 4:24 God is a spirit and they that worship him must

worship him in spirit and in truth.

John 14:16-17 And I will pray the Father, and he shall give you another Comforter, that he may abide with you for ever; Even the Spirit of truth, whom the world cannot receive, because it seeth him not, neither knoweth him: but ye know him; for he dwelleth with you and shall be in you.

John 14:26 But the Comforter, which is the Holy Ghost, whom the Father will send in my name, he shall teach you all things, and bring all things to your remembrance, whatsoever I have said unto you.

John 15:26 But when the Comforter is come, whom I will send unto you from the Father, even the Spirit of truth, which proceeedeth from the Father, he shall testify of me.

John 16:7 Nevertheless I tell you the truth; It is expedient for you that I go away: for if I go not away, the Comforter will not come unto you; but if I depart, I will send him unto you.

John 16:13 Howbeit when he, the Spirit of truth, is come, he will guide you into all truth: for he shall not speak of himself, but whatsoever he shall hear, that shall he speak and he will show you things to come.

Matthew 6:33 But seek ye first the kingdom of God, and his righteousness; and all these things shall be added unto you.

Hebrews 10:16-17 This is the covenant that I will make

with them after those days, saith the Lord, I will put my laws into their hearts, and in their minds will I write them; And their sins and iniquities will I remember no more.

1 Corinthians 4:20 For the kingdom of God is not in word, but in power.

Ephesians 2:4 But God, who is rich in mercy, for his great love wherewith he loved us.

Psalm 100:5 For the Lord is good; his mercy is everlasting; and his truth endureth to all generations.

Jude 1:21 Keep yourselves in the love of God, looking for the mercy of our Lord Jesus Christ unto eternal life.

1 Chronicles 16:34 O' give thanks unto the Lord; for he is good; for his mercy endureth for ever.

2 John 1:3 Grace be with you, mercy, and peace, from God the Father, and from the Lord Jesus Christ, the Son of the Father, in truth and love.

Isaiah 41:10 Fear thou not; for I am with thee: be not dismayed; for I am thy God: I will strengthen thee; yea, I will help thee; yea, I will uphold thee with the right hand of my righteousness.

Jeremiah 17:14 Heal me, O Lord, and I shall be healed; save me, and I shall be saved: for thou [art] my praise.

1 Peter 2:24 Who his own self bare our sins in his own body on the tree, that we, being dead to sins, should live unto righteousness: by whose stripes ye were healed.

Isaiah 53:5 But he was wounded for our transgressions, he was bruised for our iniquities: the chastisement of our peace was upon him; and with his stripes we are healed.

Jeremiah 33:6 Behold, I will bring it health and cure, and I will cure them, and will reveal unto them the abundance of peace and truth.

Psalm 103:2-4 Bless the Lord, O my soul, and forget not all his benefits.

James 5:15 And the prayer of faith shall save the sick, and the Lord shall raise him up; and if he have committed sins, they shall be forgiven him.

Matthew 10:1 And when he had called unto him his twelve disciples, he gave them power against unclean spirits, to cast them out, and to heal all manner of sickness and all manner of disease.

James 5:16 Confess your faults one to another, and pray one for another, that ye may be healed. The effectual fervent prayer of a righteous man availeth much.

3 John 1:2 Beloved, I wish above all things that thou mayest prosper and be in health, even as thy soul prospereth.

Philippians 4:19 But my God shall supply all your need according to his riches in glory by Christ Jesus.

Matthew 10:8 Heal the sick, cleanse the lepers, raise the dead, cast out devils: freely ye have received, freely give.

Proverbs 17:22 A merry heart doeth good like a medicine: but a broken spirit drieth the bones.

Deuteronomy 7:15 And the Lord will take away from thee all sickness, and will put none of the evil diseases of Egypt, which thou knowest, upon thee; but will lay them upon all them that hate thee.

Hebrews 11:6 But without faith it is impossible to please him: for he that cometh to God must believe that he is, and that he is a rewarder of them that diligently seek him.

Isaiah 54:17 No weapon that is formed against thee shall prosper; and every tongue that shall rise against thee in judgment thou shalt condemn. This is the heritage of the servants of the Lord, and their righteousness is of me, saith the Lord.

Proverbs 16:24 Pleasant words are as a honeycomb, sweet to the soul, and health to the bones.

Matthew 11:28 Come unto me, all ye that labour and are heavy laden, and I will give you rest.

Proverbs 4:20-22 My son, attend to my words; incline thine ear unto my sayings.

Isaiah 57:18 I have seen his ways, and will heal him: I will lead him also, and restore comforts unto him and to his mourners.
2 Corinthians 12:9 And he said unto me, My grace is sufficient for thee: for my strength is made perfect in

weakness. Most gladly therefore will I rather glory in my infirmities, that the power of Christ may rest upon me.

Luke 4:18 The Spirit of the Lord is upon me, because he hath anointed me to preach the gospel to the poor; he hath sent me to heal the brokenhearted, to preach deliverance to the captives, and recovering of sight to the blind, to set at liberty them that are bruised.

Psalm 6:2 Have mercy upon me, O Lord; for I am weak: O Lord, heal me; for my bones are vexed.

Hebrews 13:8 Jesus Christ the same yesterday, and to day, and for ever.

Romans 12:2 And be not conformed to this world: but be ye transformed by the renewing of your mind, that ye may prove what is that good, and acceptable, and perfect, will of God.

Romans 12:1-2 I beseech you therefore, brethren, by the mercies of God, that ye present your bodies a living sacrifice, holy, acceptable unto God, which is your reasonable service.

Numbers 6:25-26 The Lord make his face shine upon thee, and be gracious unto thee. The Lord lift up his countenance upon thee, and give thee peace.

1 Corinthians 11:1-34 Be ye followers of me, even as I also am of Christ.

Luke 10:9 And heal the sick that are therein, and say unto them, The kingdom of God is come nigh unto you.

Matthew 13:58 And he did not many mighty works there because of their unbelief.

Matthew 4:23 And Jesus went about all Galilee, teaching in their synagogues, and preaching the gospel of the kingdom, and healing all manner of sickness and all manner of disease among the people.

Jeremiah 30:17 For I will restore health unto thee, and I will heal thee of thy wounds, saith the Lord; because they called thee an Outcast, saying, This is Zion, whom no man seeketh after.

Acts 28:27 For the heart of this people is waxed gross, and their ears are dull of hearing, and their eyes have they closed; lest they should see with their eyes, and hear with their ears, and understand with their heart, and should be converted, and I should heal them.

Acts 4:30 By stretching forth thine hand to heal; and that signs and wonders may be done by the name of thy holy child Jesus.

Luke 5:17 And it came to pass on a certain day, as he was teaching, that there were Pharisees and doctors of the law sitting by, which were come out of every town of Galilee, and Judaea, and Jerusalem: and the power of the Lord was present to heal them.

Matthew 17:20 And Jesus said unto them, Because of your unbelief: for verily I say unto you, If ye have faith as a grain of mustard seed, ye shall say unto this mountain,

Remove hence to yonder place; and it shall remove; and nothing shall be impossible unto you.

Matthew 13:15 For this people's heart is waxed gross, and their ears are dull of hearing, and their eyes they have closed; lest at any time they should see with their eyes, and hear with their ears, and should understand with their heart, and should be converted, and I should heal them.

2 Corinthians 7:1 Having therefore these promises, dearly beloved, let us cleanse ourselves from all filthiness of the flesh and spirit, perfecting holiness in the fear of God.

2 Corinthians 5:7 For we walk by faith, not by sight.

2 Corinthians 1:3 Blessed be God, even the Father of our Lord Jesus Christ, the Father of mercies, and the God of all comfort.

1 Corinthians 12:9 To another faith by the same Spirit; to another the gifts of healing by the same Spirit.

Acts 10:38 How God anointed Jesus of Nazareth with the Holy Ghost and with power who went about doing good, and healing all that were oppressed of the devil; for God was with him.

John 14:27 Peace I leave with you, my peace I give unto you: not as the world giveth, give I unto you. Let not your heart be troubled, neither let it be afraid.

John 12:40 He hath blinded their eyes, and hardened their heart; that they should not see with their eyes, nor understand with their heart, and be converted, and I should heal them.

Luke 7:7 Wherefore neither thought I myself worthy to come unto thee: but say in a word, and my servant shall be healed.

Isaiah 57:19 I create the fruit of the lips; Peace, peace to him that is far off, and to him that is near, saith the Lord; and I will heal him.

Isaiah 19:22 And the Lord shall smite Egypt: he shall smite and heal it: and they shall return even to the Lord, and he shall be intreated of them, and shall heal them.

Ecclesiastes 3:11 He hath made every thing beautiful in his time: also he hath set the world in their heart, so that no man can find out the work that God maketh from the beginning to the end.

2 Chronicles 7:14 If my people, which are called by my name, shall humble themselves, and pray, and seek my face, and turn from their wicked ways; then will I hear from heaven, and will forgive their sin, and will heal their land.

2 Kings 20:8-9 And Hezekiah said unto Isaiah, What shall be the sign that the Lord will heal me, and that I shall go up into the house of the Lord the third day?

Galatians 3:14 That the blessing of Abraham might

come on the Gentiles through Jesus Christ; that we might receive the promise of the Spirit through faith.

1 Corinthians 11:1 Be ye followers of me, even as I also am of Christ.

John 4:47 When he heard that Jesus was come out of Judaea into Galilee, he went unto him, and besought him that he would come down, and heal his son: for he was at the point of death.

Luke 13:12-13 And when Jesus saw her, he called her to him, and said unto her, Woman, thou art loosed from thine infirmity. And he laid his hands on her: and immediately she was made straight, and glorified God.

Luke 14:4 And they held their peace. And he took him, and healed him, and let him go.

Luke 10:19-20 Behold, I give unto you power to tread on serpents and scorpions, and over all the power of the enemy: and nothing shall by any means hurt you.

Luke 8:48 And he said unto her, Daughter, be of good comfort: thy faith hath made thee whole; go in peace.

Be careful for nothing; but in every thing by prayer and supplication with thanksgiving let your requests be made known unto God.
Philippians 5:6

Children in the Crossfire

EXCERPT

Children in the Crossfire reveals the ongoing warfare between Lucifer and God which began before there was man. When you study the events in biblical history as a snapshot of sequential scenes, it exposes what transpired in the Kingdom of Heaven and continues in the Kingdom of Earth.

It all began with Lucifer's defiance and attempt to oust the Almighty King from His throne. Lucifer was evicted, along with the fallen angels, to the Kingdom of Earth. Realizing he wasn't going to be the king of Heaven, he set his objective to be king of Earth and stole the position from Adam through deceit. Satan rules this earthen Kingdom with the same measure of deception and your spiritual death is his desire, for it is the spirit person, born in Christ, that makes you a child of the Almighty King. We are all the target as he continuously attempts to derail us from the truth of our Most High God.

The spiritual battle is presently and actively ongoing behind the scenes in your life, and unbeknownst, playing havoc in your daily affairs. Most often when matters in life are array, we have a tendency to fault our heavenly Father. However, it isn't God but Satan, the god of this earthen Kingdom, who rules with intent to steal, kill, and destroy. Understanding this spiritual battle will enable you to deflect and denounce his attempts to place obstacles in your life.

Your stronghold in this spiritual battle is to put on the armor of God with His hedge of protection and be enveloped in your Father's arms. Be guarded and protected by the One who gives you life, loves you, desires for you to be His child, and who will give you eternity in His Kingdom. With your gift of a free will, choose the Almighty King of the Kingdom of Heaven and be released from the entrapments of this earthen ruler, so that you will no longer be a child caught in the crossfire.

Everlasting Love, God's Greatest Gift

EXCERPT

Everlasting Love, God's Greatest Gift reveals the love of the Father for His children. From the beginning of Creation, God fashioned the heavens and the earth for you with an enduring and *everlasting love*, never forgotten or forsaken. Mercy, grace, faith, blessings, promises, gifts, and supernatural power abound to the faithful children of the Almighty King. We are sons and daughters, heirs in Christ within the Kingdom of Heaven with the privilege to come before the throne of our Lord.

Everlasting Love, God's Greatest Gift presents an intimate journey into the trinity of God as the Father, the Son, and the Holy Ghost; the trinity of man created with a spirit, soul, and body; and the Kingdom of Heaven which functions with mercy, grace, and faith.

We obtain a life-altering makeover through the blood of Christ and given the gift of faith to unlock the mysteries of God's Kingdom that we may obtain His dunamis power to defeat fear, anxiety, depression, confusion, illness, disease, heartache, financial disparity, and addictions. God intends for His children to overcome and triumph in any adversity and be set free from whatever holds you captive as the result of living in a fallen world.

Take the key of faith, place it in the Kingdom lock, and turn to the truth in His Word to open a new beginning in your life today. Live as a rightful heir of the Almighty King of the Kingdom of Heaven, secure and sealed in the Father's *Everlasting Love*.

This book includes a study guide beneficial for individual or group participation. In addition, spirit topics are included with a comprehensive look at the nature, works, and position of the Son of God in the trinity of the Father, the Son, and the Holy Ghost.

ABOUT THE AUTHOR

Patricia Marlett is dedicated to writing inspirational novels for both the adult and young reader genres. With a contemporary platform, she enjoys penning plots that reflect life experiences through drama, intrigue, suspense, humor, and love. Inspirational messages are subtly woven within the endearing themes of her stories lending to heartfelt expressions from laughter to tears and always with hope and joy.

Visit Patricia at her website, www.patriciamarlett.com, to learn of her passion for writing, view her books, and for contact information.